ARTIFICIAL INTELLIGENCE

WHAT EVERYONE NEEDS TO KNOW®

ARTIFICIAL INTELLIGENCE

WHAT EVERYONE NEEDS TO KNOW®

JERRY KAPLAN

OXFORD
UNIVERSITY PRESS

OXFORD
UNIVERSITY PRESS

Oxford University Press is a department of the University of Oxford. It furthers the University's objective of excellence in research, scholarship, and education by publishing worldwide. Oxford is a registered trademark of Oxford University Press in the UK and certain other countries.

"What Everyone Needs to Know" is a registered trademark of Oxford University Press.

Published in the United States of America by Oxford University Press 198 Madison Avenue, New York, NY 10016, United States of America.

Library of Congress Cataloging-in-Publication Data
Names: Kaplan, Jerry, author.
Title: Artificial intelligence / Jerry Kaplan.
Description: Oxford: Oxford University Press, 2016. | Series: What everyone needs to know | Includes ibliographical references and index.
Identifiers: LCCN 2016001628| ISBN 9780190602390 (pbk. : alk. paper)|
ISBN 9780190602383 (hardcover : alk. paper)
Subjects: LCSH: Artificial intelligence—Social aspects—Popular works. |
Artificial intelligence—Moral and ethical aspects—Popular works. |
Classification: LCC Q335 .K36 2016 | DDC 006.3—dc23
LC record available at http://lccn.loc.gov/2016001628

Paperback printed by R.R. Donnelley, United States of America
Hardback printed by Bridgeport National Bindery, Inc., United States of America

For my mother, Mickey Kaplan
Hang in there, your eldercare robot is on the way!

CONTENTS

PREFACE   XI

ACKNOWLEDGMENTS   XV

1   Defining Artificial Intelligence   1

What is artificial intelligence?   *1*

Is AI a real science?   *4*

Can a computer ever really be smarter than a human being?   *7*

2   The Intellectual History of Artificial Intelligence   13

Where did the term artificial intelligence come from?   *13*

What were the Dartmouth conference participants hoping to accomplish?   *15*

How did early AI researchers approach the problem?   *17*

What is the "physical symbol system hypothesis"?   *20*

What is (or was) expert systems?   *22*

What is planning?   *25*

What is machine learning?   *27*

What are artificial neural networks?   *28*

How did machine learning arise?   *32*

Which approach is better, symbolic reasoning or machine learning?   *36*

What are some of the most important historical milestones in AI?   *39*

3 Frontiers of Artificial Intelligence 49

What are the main areas of research and development in AI? 49
What is robotics? 49
What is computer vision? 54
What is speech recognition? 57
What is natural language processing? 60

4 Philosophy of Artificial Intelligence 67

What is the philosophy of AI? 67
What is "strong" versus "weak" AI? 68
Can a computer "think"? 69
Can a computer have free will? 74
Can a computer be conscious? 81
Can a computer "feel"? 82

5 Artificial Intelligence and the Law 89

How will AI affect the law? 89
How will AI change the practice of law? 89
How is AI used to help lawyers? 94
What is computational law? 95
Can a computer program enter into agreements and contracts? 98
Should an intelligent agent be limited in what it is permitted to do? 98
Should people bear full responsibility for their intelligent agents? 101
Should an AI system be permitted to own property? 103
Can an AI system commit a crime? 105
Can't we just program computers to obey the law? 107
How can an AI system be held accountable for criminal acts? 107

6 The Impact of Artificial Intelligence on Human Labor   113

Are robots going to take away our jobs?   *113*

What new tasks will AI systems automate?   *116*

Which jobs are most and least at risk?   *118*

How will AI affect blue-collar workers?   *119*

How will AI affect white-collar professions?   *122*

7 The Impact of Artificial Intelligence on Social Equity   126

Who's going to benefit from this technological revolution?   *126*

Are the disruptive effects inevitable?   *127*

What's wrong with a labor-based economy?   *127*

Don't we need a thriving middle class to drive demand?   *130*

Are there alternatives to a labor-based society?   *132*

How can we distribute future assets more equitably?   *132*

How can we support the unemployed without government handouts?   *134*

Why should people work if they could live comfortably without doing so?   *136*

8 Possible Future Impacts of Artificial Intelligence   138

Is progress in AI accelerating?   *138*

What is the "singularity"?   *138*

When might the singularity occur?   *141*

Is runaway superintelligence a legitimate concern?   *144*

Will artificially intelligent systems ever get loose and go wild?   *146*

How can we minimize the future risks?   *148*

What are the benefits and risks of making computers and robots that act like people?   *150*

How are our children likely to regard AI systems?   *152*

Will I ever be able to upload myself into a computer?   *153*

INDEX   **157**

PREFACE

Books in the Oxford University Press series *What Everyone Needs to Know* are intended as concise and balanced primers on complex issues of current or impending relevance to society in a question-and-answer format. This volume focuses on artificial intelligence, commonly abbreviated AI. After more than five decades of research, the field of AI is poised to transform the way we live, work, socialize, and even how we regard our place in the universe.

Most books on AI are typically introductory textbooks, a review of work in some subfield or institution, or the prognostications of an individual researcher or futurist (like me). In contrast, I intend the current volume as a succinct introduction to some of the complex social, legal, and economic issues raised by the field that are likely to impact our society over the next few decades.

Rather than focus on technological details, I attempt to provide a synoptic overview of the basic issues and arguments on all sides of important debates, such as whether machines are ever likely to exceed human intelligence, how they might be granted legal rights, and what impact the new generation of learning, flexible robots may have on labor markets and income inequality. These are controversial subjects, and there is a large and vibrant community of scholars engaged in vigorous debate on many of the questions I will address here. I do not attempt a comprehensive review of the literature or provide equal time to the myriad viewpoints. Naturally, my personal opinions are not universally shared, but to help you sort out my viewpoint from others, I lapse into first person to signal when I am presenting the former.

Where appropriate, I use current projects or applications to illuminate and enliven the discussion, but since progress in AI tends to move very quickly, I do not attempt to provide a complete survey of the current state of the art—which would inevitably be incomplete and quickly go stale (there's a decidedly long delay between manuscript and publication). Instead, I provide pointers to some of the more notable thinkers and projects as entry points for readers interested in a deeper dive. As a result, theorists and practitioners working in the field may find my treatment more casual than they are accustomed to in professional journals and forums, for which I apologize in advance.

In summary, this book is not intended to convey original research, cover the selected topics in depth, or serve as a textbook for emerging practitioners. Instead, it is meant to be a convenient way for curious nontechnical readers to get a condensed and accessible introduction to the topic and the potential future impact of this important technology.

With these preliminaries out of the way, let's warm up by answering the question *Why should you read this book?*

Recent advances in robotics, perception, and machine learning, supported by accelerating improvements in computer technology, have enabled a new generation of systems that rival or exceed human capabilities in limited domains or on specific tasks. These systems are far more autonomous than most people realize. They can learn from their own experience and take actions never contemplated by their designers. The widely accepted wisdom that "computers can only do what people program them to do" no longer applies.

Advances in the intellectual and physical capabilities of machines will change the way we live, work, play, seek a mate, educate our young, and care for our elderly. They will also upend our labor markets, reshuffle our social order, and strain our private and public institutions. Whether we regard these machines as conscious or unwitting, revere them as a new form of life, or dismiss them as mere clever appliances is beside the point. They are likely to play an increasingly critical and intimate role in many aspects of our lives.

The emergence of systems capable of independent thought and action raises serious questions about just whose interests they are permitted to serve, and what limits our society should place on their creation and use. Deep ethical questions that have bedeviled philosophers for ages will suddenly arrive on the steps of our courthouses. Can a machine be held accountable for its actions? Should intelligent systems enjoy independent rights and responsibilities, or are they simply property? Who should be held responsible when a self-driving car kills a pedestrian? Can your personal robot hold your place in line or be compelled to testify against you? If it turns out to be possible to upload your mind into a machine, is that still you? The answers may surprise you.

Grappling with these issues will be difficult because current public perception is shaped more by Hollywood blockbusters than practical reality. Instead, we should look for guidance to our historical relationships with slaves, animals, and corporations as well as to our evolving views on the treatment of women, children, and the disabled.

Over the next few decades, AI will stretch our social fabric to the limit. Whether the future will be a new age of unprecedented prosperity and freedom as depicted in *Star Trek* or a perpetual struggle of humans against machines as portrayed in *Terminator* will largely depend on our own actions. Here's everything you need to know to help shape our future.

ACKNOWLEDGMENTS

I am indebted to several readers and reviewers for their thoughtful comments and suggestions, most notably Nils Nilsson, Michael Steger, and Peter Hart.

I would like to thank my acquiring editor, Jeremy Lewis, and editorial assistant, Anna Langley at Oxford University Press for inviting me to write this book, as well as my project manager Prabhu Chinnasamy at Newgen Publishing & Data Services in India.

My literary agent Emma Parry and her colleagues at Janklow & Nesbit Associates in New York did an exemplary job of handling rights negotiations and providing invaluable advice. As noted above, Michael Steger, Contracts Director, went above and beyond by reading and commenting on an early draft of the manuscript.

My copy editor, Robin DuBlanc did a fabulous job of sharpening up the prose—she's a wonderful linguistic makeover artist. "And so on," not "etc." Got it.

Also thanks to Anna Zhang, Senior Vice President and co-founder, and Kelly Zheng Rights Manager of Cheers Publishing, Beijing, for their interest in promoting my books in China.

Rodney Brooks and Sue Sokoloski of Rethink Robotics, Inc. kindly permitted me to use a picture of their amazing robot "Baxter" for the cover photo.

And of course I'm grateful to my delightful wife Michelle Pettigrew Kaplan for her patience while I hid away working on this manuscript!

1

DEFINING ARTIFICIAL INTELLIGENCE

What is artificial intelligence?

That's an easy question to ask and a hard one to answer—for two reasons. First, there's little agreement about what intelligence is. Second, there's scant reason to believe that machine intelligence bears much relationship to human intelligence, at least so far.

There are many proposed definitions of artificial intelligence (AI), each with its own slant, but most are roughly aligned around the concept of creating computer programs or machines capable of behavior we would regard as intelligent if exhibited by humans. John McCarthy, a founding father of the discipline, described the process in 1955 as "that of making a machine behave in ways that would be called intelligent if a human were so behaving."[1]

But this seemingly sensible approach to characterizing AI is deeply flawed. Consider, for instance, the difficulty of defining, much less measuring, human intelligence. Our cultural predilection for reducing things to numeric measurements that facilitate direct comparison often creates a false patina of objectivity and precision. And attempts to quantify something as subjective and abstract as intelligence is clearly in this category. Young Sally's IQ is seven points higher than Johnny's? Please—find some fairer way to decide who gets that precious last slot in kindergarten. For just one example of attempts to tease this over-simplification apart, consider the controversial framework of developmental psychologist Howard Gardner, who proposes an eight-dimensional theory of intelligence ranging from "musical–rhythmic" through "bodily–kinesthetic" to "naturalistic."[2]

Nonetheless, it's meaningful to say that one person is smarter than another, at least within many contexts. And there are certain markers of intelligence that are widely accepted and highly correlated with other indicators. For instance, how quickly and accurately students can add and subtract lists of numbers is extensively used as a measure of logical and quantitative abilities, not to mention attention to detail. But does it make any sense to apply this standard to a machine? A $1 calculator will beat any human being at this task hands down, even without hands. Prior to World War II, a "calculator" was a skilled professional—usually a female, interestingly enough, since women were believed to be able to perform this painstaking work more meticulously than most men. So is speed of calculation an indicator that machines possess superior ·intelligence? Of course not.

Complicating the task of comparing human and machine intelligence is that most AI researchers would agree that *how* you approach the problem is as important as *whether* you solve it. To understand why, consider a simple computer program that plays the game of tic-tac-toe (you may know this as noughts and crosses), where players alternate placing Xs and Os on a three-by-three grid until one player completes three in a row, column, or diagonal (or all spaces are filled, in which case the game is a draw).

There are exactly 255,168 unique games of tic-tac-toe, and in today's world of computers, it's a fairly simple matter to generate all possible game sequences, mark the ones that are wins, and play a perfect game just by looking up each move in a table.[3] But most people wouldn't accept such a trivial program as artificially intelligent. Now imagine a different approach: a computer program with no preconceived notion of what the rules are, that observes humans playing the game and learns not only what it means to win but what strategies are most successful. For instance, it might learn that after one player gets two in a row, the other player should always make a blocking move, or that occupying three corners with blanks between them frequently results in a win. Most people would credit the program with AI, particularly since it was able to acquire the needed expertise without any guidance or instruction.

Now, not all games, and certainly not all interesting problems, are susceptible to solution by enumeration like tic-tac-toe.[4] By contrast, chess has approximately 10^{120} unique games, vastly exceeding the number of atoms in the universe.[5] So, much of AI research can be seen as an attempt to find acceptable solutions to problems that are not amenable to definitive analysis or enumeration for any number of theoretical and practical reasons. And yet, this characterization alone is not sufficient—many statistical methods meet this criterion but would hardly qualify as AI.

Nonetheless, there is an unintuitive yet real practical equivalence between selecting an answer from an enormously large proliferation of possibilities and intuiting an answer through insight and creativity. A common formulation of this paradox is that enough monkeys at enough keyboards will eventually type out the complete works of Shakespeare, but in a more modern context, every possible musical performance of a given length can be represented as one of a finite collection of MP3 files. Is the ability to select that particular music file from the list an equivalent creative act to recording that selection? Surely it's not the same, but perhaps these skills are equally deserving of our applause.

When scoring students' performances on sums, we don't take into account how they performed the work—we presume they used only their native brains and the necessary tools like pencil and paper. So why do we care when we substitute a machine as the test subject? Because we take it for granted that a human performing this task is using certain innate or learned abilities that in principle can be brought to bear on a broad range of comparable problems of interest. However, we lack confidence that a machine demonstrating the same or superior performance on this task indicates anything of the kind.

But there's another problem with using human capabilities as a yardstick for AI. Machines are able to perform lots of tasks that people can't do at all, and many such performances certainly feel like displays of intelligence. A security program may suspect a cyber attack based on an unusual pattern of data access requests in a span of just five hundred milliseconds; a tsunami warning system may sound an alarm based on barely perceptible changes in ocean heights that mirror complex undersea geography; a drug discovery program may propose a novel admixture by finding a previously unnoticed pattern of molecular arrangements in successful cancer treatment compounds. The behavior exhibited by systems like these, which will become ever more common in the near future, doesn't lend itself to comparison with human capabilities. Nonetheless, we are likely to regard such systems as artificially intelligent.

Another marker of intelligence is how gracefully we fail. Everyone (including intelligent machines) makes mistakes, but some mistakes are more reasonable than others. Understanding and respecting our own limits and making plausible errors are hallmarks of expertise. Consider the difficult challenge of translating spoken into written language. When a court stenographer accidentally transcribes "She made a mistake that led to his death" as "She made him a steak, which led to his death," the lapse seems excusable.[6] But when Google Voice proposes "wreak a nice beach you sing calm incense" for "recognize speech using common sense," it invites ridicule, in part because we expect it to be more familiar with its own wheelhouse.[7]

Is AI a real science?

Over the past few decades, the field of AI has grown from its infancy—playing with toy problems like tic-tac-toe and chess—into its professional adolescence—striking out for parts unknown, acquiring new skills, exploring the real world, and seeking to discover its own limits. But will it ever mature into a full-fledged scientific discipline?

To briefly wade into deep waters of speculation, many fields get their sea legs, or make substantial headway, only after some mathematical formalism emerges to provide a solid theoretical foundation. For example, the non-Euclidian geometry of Bernard Riemann set the stage for Einstein's theories of the curvature of space-time. Closer to home, Claude Shannon's remarkable 1937 MIT master's thesis, in which he proposed for the first time that electronic circuits could be modeled by Boolean algebra—more commonly known as binary arithmetic—laid the groundwork for modern computer science.[8] (It is because of him that we speak today of computers processing "zeros and ones.") Before that, electrical engineers mostly cobbled together odd components into circuits, then measured what they did. My gadget rectified alternating current (AC) into direct current (DC) better than yours, but don't ask me why.

Today's AI conferences occasionally have a similar feel, with one group's algorithms besting another's in an escalating cavalcade of annual bake-offs. But is intelligence susceptible to theoretical analysis? Does it await a simple "aha" moment by some mathematically minded engineer? This question is at the crux of whether AI is a distinct discipline or simply the Lady Gaga of computer science—performing numbers swaddled in gaudy, anthropomorphic costumes, capturing the popular imagination and the lion's share of the financial support, a carny sideshow prone to occasional hucksterism and hubris, leaving us to wonder whether it's real or simply a parlor trick.

Which leads me to my personal view of the meaning of AI. The essence of AI—indeed, the essence of intelligence—is the ability to make appropriate generalizations in a timely fashion based on limited data. The broader the domain of application, the quicker conclusions are drawn with minimal information, the more intelligent the behavior. If the same program that learns tic-tac-toe can learn *any* board game, all the better. If it can also learn to recognize faces, diagnose medical conditions, and compose music in the style of Bach, I believe we would agree that it's artificially intelligent (there are individual programs that passably perform each of these tasks today). Whether it does so the same way people do, and whether it appears to be self-aware as people are, would seem to be irrelevant.

An important key to making good generalizations is to bring to bear the broadest available context. When you decide to avoid driving a particular route because it often gets backed up, today is a holiday, the weather is good, and that route is the best way to the beach, you are performing just this sort of generalization. When your mail program suggests adding a conference call to your calendar based on the text of an e-mail you received, shifting the time because the sender is in a different time zone, interpreting "next Tuesday" as eight days away instead of tomorrow, and linking the calendar entry to the sender's record in your contacts for your convenience, it is engaging in a similar process of generalizing from multiple sources of knowledge. When that same program stops making such suggestions because you routinely decline, it is also generalizing based on context. In fact, learning can be viewed as a process of performing temporally sequential generalizations, by taking prior experience into account in future analyses, just as reasoning by analogy is a matter of using knowledge from one domain as a novel context with which to generalize about another. Sometimes you have to go pretty far afield for guidance when confronting fresh challenges, but if done judiciously, the results can seem very intelligent indeed. There are tantalizing hints that broadened context may be the basis of our own consciousness, as I will discuss shortly. Perhaps breadth breeds brilliance.

Numerous researchers are attempting to plumb the depths of the human mind (or at least skim the surface) by studying the detailed structure of the brain, in part to unravel how we perform these remarkable cognitive feats. The mystery they face is how relatively straightforward and uniform biological units (neurons), through their interconnections, could possibly account for such varied feats as storing memories, processing visual information, controlling our bodies, producing emotions, guiding our behavior, and generating our qualitative sense of self. As inexplicable as it seems, this appears to be the case. So who's to say that a comparably simple computer program, with free rein over sufficient computing resources and input, can't do the same?

So will artificially intelligent computers suddenly "come alive," as is often depicted in fiction? Don't hold your breath. Having spent much of my life mucking about in the innards of increasingly sophisticated AI programs, I have yet to see a wisp of evidence that we may be heading in that direction, at least for the foreseeable future. More likely, the tasks that we deem to require human ingenuity are simply more susceptible to automation than we would care to believe. Intelligence, as a coherent concept amenable to formal analysis, measurement, and duplication, may simply be an illusion.

AI may not be a hard science in the sense of physics or chemistry, where theories and hypotheses are subject to objective confirmation, though it may ultimately get there.[9] What qualifies as AI, as opposed to merely clever programming or engineering, may be open to debate, but we should take care not to let this lack of agreement distract us from an important truth: this new technology will impact a great many things that we hold dear, from our livelihoods to our sense of self. We may not be able to define AI just yet, but in the meantime I'm confident that most people feel, as U.S. Supreme Court justice Potter Stewart famously said of pornography, "I know it when I see it."[10]

Can a computer ever really be smarter than a human being?

In a word, yes—but most likely in limited ways. It's possible that at some point in the future public sentiment will have shifted sufficiently to accept the idea that computers are in general superior to humans in some fairly broad classes of intellectual tasks, but this doesn't mean that machines will dominate or obsolete us, as I will explain later. Cars can "outrun" us, ATMs can count bills faster than we can, cameras can see in the dark, but we don't regard any of these as threatening our primacy. Computer programs can already play games, scan a crowd for familiar faces, and recommend movies as well or better than we can, yet few people are intimidated by these competencies. If or when robots can perform brain surgery, paint houses, cut hair, and help us find our lost keys, I expect we will see them as incredibly useful tools that can accomplish tasks that previously required native human intelligence, so the temptation to speak of them also as "smart" will be difficult to resist.

But in doing so, we should be careful to circumscribe what we mean by this. Intelligence, as we might use the word for machines, is likely to apply to well-defined activities in which the goals can be easily specified and measured (Is the grass mowed? Did I get to my destination on time? Will it rain tomorrow? Are my taxes filed correctly?), but not to others in which success is more subjective (Which dress looks better on me? What college is the right choice for me? Should I marry Bill? What would life be like if the Nazis had won World War II? How can I cheer up my child after she loses a soccer match?).

History is replete with misguided prognostications about what computers will never be able to do, so I'm skating on thin ice by offering up examples. No doubt computer programs can be written that will at least plausibly attempt to answer these sorts of subjective or judgmental questions, but I expect that their answers will not be regarded as preferable to, more perceptive than, or wiser than those of humans.

While today the prospect that we may eventually regard machines as "more intelligent" than humans may seem uncomfortable, by the time it happens it will likely be no more remarkable than many prior technological advances anticipated with horror, such as in vitro fertilization ("test-tube babies"), the supposedly numbing and dumbing effects of television on children, and (my personal favorite) the menace of recorded music.[11] That said, AI researchers are hardly free of sin. They have been notoriously overoptimistic, as critics have been quick to point out (most notably, philosopher Hubert Dreyfus).[12]

Note that this question is distinct from whether computers will supplant humans in all (as opposed to many) current jobs and activities.[13] There are plenty of things we do because we enjoy them, often including work itself. As a student of mine once sarcastically (I hope) responded to an essay question asking why we program computers to play chess, "To save us from the drudgery of having to play chess ourselves."

To understand why computers are likely to exceed human intelligence in a variety of practical applications, it's helpful to start with the straightforward observation that computers surpass human capabilities in many tasks today, including some that we might have believed require human intelligence. Driving cars, playing *Jeopardy*, predicting wars, and summarizing press releases are but a few examples.[14] Now consider the question of why we think of these as separate capabilities. Bundle enough of them together in a single entity, and the result could appear to be generally intelligent, even if it doesn't do some things well (yet), such as write novels.[15] But this appearance will be little more than a mirage.

Does adding more accomplishments to this list mean that machines are getting more intelligent in the human sense? For some insight into this question, consider your smartphone. It replaces a wide variety of formerly distinct tools—cameras, cell phones, music players, navigation systems, even flashlights and magnifying glasses—telescoping them into a single device. But do you feel that your phone gets "smarter" each time you download a new app? I suspect not. No matter how capable it becomes, it's still the information-processing analogue of the Swiss Army knife—lots of useful tools cleverly integrated into one easily carried appliance.

That said, there's also an argument to be made that many of these functions may consolidate. The methods that underlie each of these accomplishments can begin to coalesce into a shrinking collection of techniques with ever more general applicability. This tendency for technologies to consolidate may be surprising, given the seemingly endless parade of new gadget introductions, but much of it takes place out of sight and under the hood. This same trend is evident in the history of software. For instance, there was a time when every company that wanted to store information in a computer had to essentially write its own database management system designed for the particulars of its own data. As commonalities soon became evident, several competing standard representations arose (most notably the networked and hierarchical data models), which themselves were ultimately supplanted by the relational database model commonly used today for most commercial applications.[16]

As I've noted previously, none of this implies that future computers will necessarily perform these tasks as we do. In later chapters I will cover machine learning in more detail, but one of the biggest surprises of the past few years has been that relatively simple statistical methods, when supplied with a sufficiently large number of examples, are capable of tasks that would otherwise appear to require comprehension and insight. For example, machine translation of one human language to another—which was stuck at a poor level of performance for many years—has made dramatic strides now that large numbers of successfully translated texts are available.[17] It's perhaps a bit disquieting to realize that every time you ask a question or perform a search, you are making the computers that serve up the answer incrementally smarter and more attentive to our human needs.

With their superior speed, accuracy, and memory capacity, computers may more effectively perform tasks like playing chess or translating text by searching for answers, whereas humans may perform better using other techniques. But as automated methods continue to chip away at a long list of abilities previously considered the unique and sole province of humans, the distinction between human and machine intelligence for the average person may blur into irrelevance. Sometimes the best man or woman for the job may be a machine.

Notes

1. J. McCarthy, M. L. Minsky, N. Rochester, and C. E. Shannon, "A Proposal for the Dartmouth Summer Research Project on Artificial Intelligence," 1955, http://www-formal.stanford.edu/jmc/history/dartmouth/dartmouth.html.
2. Howard Gardner, *Frames of Mind: The Theory of Multiple Intelligences* (New York, NY: Basic Books, 1983).
3. The number of unique games of tic-tac-toe is bounded by 9 factorial (9! = 362,880), but many end before the board is filled. If you take into account all the symmetries and rotations, the list condenses to only 138, 91 of which are won by the player making the initial move, 44 by the other player, and 3 that are draws. So go first.
4. Approaches that enumerate the set of cases or solutions are called "extensional"; those that describe such sets are called "intensional."
5. Diego Rasskin-Gutman, Deborah Klosky (translator), *Chess Metaphors: Artificial Intelligence and the Human Mind* (Cambridge, MA: MIT Press, 2009).
6. J. A. Wines, *Mondegreens: A Book of Mishearings* (London: Michael O'Mara Books, 2007).
7. Henry Lieberman, Alexander Faaborg, Waseem Daher, José Espinosa, "How to Wreck a Nice Beach You Sing Calm Incense," MIT Media Laboratory, in *Proceedings of the 10th International Conference on Intelligent User Interfaces* (New York: ACM, 2005), 278–80. Ironically, I hesitate to think of how this example will be expressed in foreign-language versions of this work. If you're reading this in Mandarin and the paragraph doesn't make any sense, please bear in mind that the translator was handed an impossible task.
8. Claude Elwood Shannon, "A symbolic analysis of relay and switching circuits," master's thesis, Dept. of Electrical Engineering, Massachusetts Institute of Technology, 1940.
9. More precisely, theories must be potentially subject to falsification, not verification, to be considered hard science. For instance, see http://www.amazon.com/Logic-Scientific-Discovery-Routledge-Classics/dp/0415278449/.

10. Peter Lattman "The Origins of Justice Stewart's 'I Know It When I See It,'" September 27, 2007, LawBlog, *Wall Street Journal Online*. Or see 378 U.S. 184 (1964).

11. John Philip Sousa, "The Menace of Mechanical Music," *Appleton's* 8 (1906), http://explorepahistory.com/odocument.php?docId= 1-4-1A1.

12. See http://www.amazon.com/What-Computers-Still-Cant-Artificial/dp/ 0262540673.

13. See http://www.makeuseof.com/tag/6-human-jobs-computers-will-never-replace/.

14. On predicting wars, see H. Hegre, J. Karlsen, H. M. Nygård, H. Strand, and H. Urdal, "Predicting Armed Conflict, 2010–2050," *International Studies Quarterly* 57 (2013): 250–70, doi: 10.1111/isqu.12007, http:// onlinelibrary.wiley.com/doi/10.1111/isqu.12007/ full.

15. As of this writing, programs exist that write plausible novels. See http://www.businessinsider.com/novels-written-by-computers-2014-11.

16. For a short survey, see "A Brief History of Database Systems," http://www.comphist.org/computing_history/new_page_9.htm. Relational databases are in fact another example of a mathematical formalism (the theory of relations) providing a firm theoretical foundation for a previously ad hoc engineering practice.

17. See http://en.wikipedia.org/wiki/Statistical_machine_translation.

2

THE INTELLECTUAL HISTORY
OF ARTIFICIAL INTELLIGENCE

Where did the term artificial intelligence *come from?*

The first use of "artificial intelligence" can be attributed to a specific individual—John McCarthy, in 1956 an assistant professor of mathematics at Dartmouth College in Hanover, New Hampshire. Along with three other, more senior researchers (Marvin Minsky of Harvard, Nathan Rochester of IBM, and Claude Shannon of Bell Telephone Laboratories), McCarthy proposed a summer conference on the topic to take place at Dartmouth. Several prominent researchers attended, many of whom went on to make fundamental contributions to the field.

The original conference funding proposal to the Rockefeller Foundation stated, "The study is to proceed on the basis of the conjecture that every aspect of learning or any other feature of intelligence can in principle be so precisely described that a machine can be made to simulate it. An attempt will be made to find how to make machines use language, form abstractions and concepts, solve kinds of problems now reserved for humans, and improve themselves."[1]

McCarthy selected the term *artificial intelligence* for the conference in part to distinguish his and his colleagues' work from the more established field of cybernetics—"the scientific study of control and communication in the animal and the machine"—which approached its subject primarily from the perspective of how animals and machines use feedback to adjust and correct their behavior.[2] In contrast, McCarthy and many of his colleagues were aficionados of symbolic logic, the branch of mathematics that deals with representing concepts and statements as symbols, then defines various transformations to manipulate these symbols to reason deductively from hypotheses to conclusions (or inductively from conclusions back to hypotheses). For instance, symbols might represent "Socrates," "man," and "mortal," as well as the statements "Socrates is a man," and "All men are mortal." From this, you could formally derive that "Socrates is mortal." Most mathematicians who studied symbolic logic were concerned not with actually proving statements like this or applying the techniques to specific problems, but rather with studying the theoretical properties of logical systems—such as delineating what such systems can and can't do.

But the advent of electronic computing devices raised the possibility that all this theory might actually have a practical use. After all, computers had proved their mettle during World War II as an efficient way to calculate ballistics tables (how to aim big guns) and to encrypt, decrypt, and even break secret codes. Placed in this historical context, the Dartmouth conference could be seen as an attempt to expand the use of computers beyond crunching numbers and processing data to manipulating symbols. McCarthy himself went on to create a number of seminal inventions in the field, most notably the elegant programming language LISP, which stood for "list processing," not a speech impediment; as I recall from my conversations with him years later, his diction was perfectly clear, though he definitely gave off that crazy genius vibe pioneered by Albert Einstein and perfected by Christopher Lloyd as Dr. Emmett Brown in *Back to the Future*.

What were the Dartmouth conference participants hoping to accomplish?

The Dartmouth proposal covered a surprisingly broad range of topics, including neuron nets, a precursor of some of today's most powerful AI techniques, and the processing of human language by computer, both of which I will describe shortly.

Some of the more interesting statements in the proposal illustrate the mindset of the participants. For instance, it's clear that McCarthy believed that a computer could simulate many or all advanced human cognitive functions. As he put it, "The speeds and memory capacities of present computers may be insufficient to simulate many of the higher functions of the human brain, but the major obstacle is not lack of machine capacity, but our inability to write programs taking full advantage of what we have.... Probably a truly intelligent machine will carry out activities which may best be described as self-improvement.... A fairly attractive and yet clearly incomplete conjecture is that the difference between creative thinking and unimaginative competent thinking lies in the injection of some randomness. The randomness must be guided by intuition to be efficient. In other words, the educated guess or the hunch include controlled randomness in otherwise orderly thinking."[3] All these somewhat off-the-cuff remarks presaged important areas of study within the field.

But in some regards, the proposal was widely off the mark. For instance, it included the wildly overoptimistic projection "We think that a significant advance can be made in one or more of these problems if a carefully selected group of scientists work on it together for a summer."[4] While it's not clear what, if anything, was actually accomplished at this conference (the promised final report was never delivered), this is perhaps the first example of practitioners in the field making overly optimistic promises and projections about what would be achieved and how long it would take the initiative to accomplish its goals. Largely as a result, and in contrast to more pedestrian fields, funding and therefore progress in AI has gone through several highly visible cycles of boom and bust, creating periodic so-called "AI winters" in which the field was substantially out of favor with governmental and industrial patrons. Indeed, the field seems to attract the enmity of many deep thinkers, such as noted philosophers Hubert Dreyfus and John Searle (both at the University of California at Berkeley).[5]

But perhaps the most remarkable, albeit overlooked, result of the Dartmouth proposal is the improbable and most likely unintentional success of the term *artificial intelligence* in attracting interest and attention far beyond its academic roots. Nothing in McCarthy's life suggests that he harbored a hidden interest or talent for coining brilliant marketing slogans, yet his choice of this particular moniker has sparked an enduring fascination by the press, public, and entertainment media—an achievement that eludes all but the most accomplished advertising professionals. Little more than speculation and wishful thinking ties the actual work in AI to the mysterious workings of the human mind—in practice it's an engineering discipline whose relationship to biological organisms is mostly metaphorical and inspirational, at least at this stage. (There are related fields, notably cognitive science and computational neuroscience, which have a stronger claim to biological relevance.)

To better understand how the aspirational connection between machine and human intelligence clouds and colors our understanding of this important technology, imagine the confusion and controversy that powered flight might have suffered if airplanes were described from the start as "artificial birds." This nomenclature would invite distracting comparisons between aviation and avians, sparking philosophical debates as to whether airplanes can really be said to "fly" as birds do, or merely simulate flying. (The parallel here is the ongoing debates as to whether machines can really think or just simulate thinking. And the answer is the same: it depends on what you mean.) Yes, airplanes have wings, which were plausibly inspired by bird wings, but they don't flap or fold and the propulsion system is completely different, as is their range, altitude, and just about everything else about them. If this misplaced framing had persisted, there might have been conferences of experts and pundits worrying about what will happen when planes learn to make nests, develop the ability to design and build their own progeny, forage for fuel to feed their young, and so on. As ridiculous as this sounds, its similarity to the current wave of concern about superintelligent machines and runaway AI posing a threat to humanity is stronger than a casual observer might expect. Little or nothing in the field of AI today, other than wild speculation, supports these concerns—at least for the foreseeable future. And if it ever does, we're likely to have plenty of warning.

Had McCarthy chosen a more pedestrian term that didn't suggest a challenge to human dominance or cognition, like "symbolic processing" or "analytical computing," you might not be reading this book right now. Progress in the field might have merely seemed like what it is—the continuing advance of automation.

How did early AI researchers approach the problem?

After the Dartmouth conference, interest in the field (and opposition to it in a few quarters) grew quickly. Researchers began working on a variety of tasks, from proving theorems to playing games. Some of the early groundbreaking work involved highly visible accomplishments such as Arthur Samuel's 1959 checkers player.[6] This remarkable program demonstrated to the world the novel proposition that a computer could be programmed to learn to play a game better than its creator. It could improve its performance by playing and could do something that humans could not—play against itself to practice— eventually reaching advanced amateur status. Allen Newell and Herbert Simon (who later won a Nobel Prize in economics) created the Logic Theory Machine in 1956, proving most of the theorems in Whitehead and Russell's 1910 formalization of mathematics, *Principia Mathematica*.[7] A few years later, the same team built the General Problem Solver, which was designed explicitly to mimic the observed behavior of human subjects in trying to solve logic and other problems.[8]

Many demonstration systems of the day focused on so-called toy problems, limiting their applicability to some simplified or self-contained world, such as games or logic. This was partly motivated by the theory that many scientific advances occur when assumptions can be simplified or phenomena studied in isolation. (For instance, the barren and relatively sparse natural environment in the Galápagos Islands was a critical aid to Darwin in observing the effects of natural selection.) It was also motivated by necessity—computers of the time were almost laughably feeble compared to today's. A typical smartphone today is literally over 1 million times more powerful than the computing devices available to the early AI researchers.

But this same expedient opened the field to criticism and even ridicule. Herbert Dreyfus excoriated the entire enterprise in a 1965 report entitled "Alchemy and Artificial Intelligence," causing an uproar among AI researchers.[9] He later drolly observed, "The first man to climb a tree could claim tangible progress toward reaching the moon."[10]

But starting in the mid-1960s, the field found a wealthy patron in the Advanced Research Projects Agency of the U.S. Department of Defense (now called the Defense Advanced Research Projects Agency, or DARPA). Following an investment theory that it should fund centers of excellence as opposed to specific projects, the organization poured millions of dollars annually into three nascent academic AI labs at MIT, Stanford University, and Carnegie Mellon University as well as some notable commercial research labs such as SRI International. Another prominent research center was located at the University of Edinburgh in the U.K.

The consistent flow of money despite little in the way of expected deliverables fostered a freewheeling intellectual culture.

Optimism abounded, and successive waves of graduate students fell over each other in an effort to stand out from the pack by demonstrating some amazing new thing that computers could be shown to do, occasionally without adequately framing the concept's limitations and drawbacks. At SRI, a team of researchers integrated the state of the art in computer vision, mapping, planning, learning, and error recovery (among others) to build Shakey the robot, one of the first autonomous vehicles—Shakey, a rolling cart, could navigate around the relatively controlled environment of SRI's labs and halls. Despite operating exclusively in this relatively simple and artificial domain, Shakey gave the world one of the earliest glimpses of a real AI program embodied in a mobile form that anyone could comprehend. When Shakey, its way blocked by a chair, paused to formulate its next action, was it merely crunching numbers or was it lost in thought? Was *Life* magazine right to refer to Shakey as the "first electronic person" in 1970?[11]

Another development that illustrated the significant progress being made but also how the field was prone to hype was Terry Winograd's MIT PhD thesis. His demonstration program, named SHRDLU after the second column of letters on a typesetting machine, answered questions in natural language (plain English) and moved blocks around in a virtual world.[12] This masterful work brought together recent progress in syntax, semantics, question answering, dialog, logic, knowledge representation, and computer graphics to create an astonishing display of apparent machine intelligence, bearing the implicit promise that we might soon be able to engage in dialog with computers as intellectual peers. The following provides a sense of how remarkably lifelike SHRDLU's dialogs appeared:[13]

PERSON: Pick up a big red block.
COMPUTER: OK.
PERSON: Grasp the pyramid.
COMPUTER: I don't understand which pyramid you mean.

PERSON (CHANGING THEIR MIND): Find a block which is taller than the one you are holding and put it into the box.

COMPUTER: By "it," I assume you mean the block which is taller than the one I am holding.

COMPUTER: OK.

PERSON: What does the box contain?

COMPUTER: The blue pyramid and the blue block.

PERSON: What is the pyramid supported by?

COMPUTER: The box.

PERSON: How many blocks are not in the box?

COMPUTER: Four of them.

PERSON: Is at least one of them narrower than the one which I told you to pick up?

COMPUTER: Yes, the red cube.

As impressive as this dialog is, what it fails to communicate is just how fragile question-answering systems like this were at the time, both in terms of what they could discuss and how limited the inputs had to be. Still, just about anyone—whether an AI researcher or member of the general public—could be forgiven for suspecting that human-level AI was just around the corner. (Indeed, Winograd's thesis was a prime inspiration for my choice of a career in AI and, more specifically, for my own PhD work in natural language query systems.) But the plain fact is that question-answering systems, though greatly improved, have failed to live up to this promise, even today. Winograd, who went on to a distinguished career as a professor at Stanford University, essentially switched fields from AI to human-computer interfaces (known as HCI).[14]

What is the "Physical Symbol System Hypothesis"?

Underlying SHRDLU was a language called Planner, designed by Carl Hewitt, also a graduate student at MIT.[15] Planner was one of the intellectual successors to Logic Theorist, following in the tradition of using mathematical logic, broadly construed, as a basis for AI. This approach, prominent at the Dartmouth conference, remained the primary focus of AI researchers through much of the 1970s and 1980s, though it has mostly fallen out of favor since (for reasons that I will explain shortly). Perhaps its most articulate formulation was by Newell and Simon themselves. In accepting their joint 1975 Turing Award—a prestigious honor in computer science—they defined what they called the "physical symbol system hypothesis." Quoting from their award acceptance lecture, "Symbols lie at the root of intelligent action, which is, of course, the primary topic of artificial intelligence. . . . A physical symbol system is a machine that produces through time an evolving collection of symbol structures." They go on to delineate the hypothesis:

> A physical symbol system has the necessary and sufficient means for general intelligent action. By "necessary" we mean that any system that exhibits general intelligence will prove upon analysis to be a physical symbol system. By "sufficient" we mean that any physical symbol system of sufficient size can be organized further to exhibit general intelligence. By "general intelligent action" we wish to indicate . . . the same scope of intelligence as we see in human action: . . . in any real situation behavior appropriate to the ends of the system and adaptive to the demands of the environment can occur, within some limits of speed and complexity.[16]

While their characterization of the dominant approach to AI at the time is insightful and inspiring, in retrospect it suffers from a significant defect. Despite the fact that it is presented as an empirical hypothesis, it is not, by itself, subject to confirmation or refutation. Alternative approaches to AI not based on anything like their proposed methodology could be equally or more effective in achieving their aspirations for the field, calling into question whether "symbols lie at the root of intelligent action." Yet, their rebuttal could be that an equivalent (or better) physical symbol system solution may exist; it just hasn't been developed yet. In other words, their description of the field is a little like a prescription for how to address a golf ball in order to drive it as straight and as far as possible (keep your head steady and your eye on the ball, use your leading arm for power and your following arm for control). Equating this with the optimal (or only) way to play the game would seem to overreach—you may have a different approach and yet become the world's best golfer. And indeed, at least one alternative approach (machine learning) to AI that has no obvious relationship to their hypothesis did emerge, but not before another major wave of systems targeted at practical applications that followed the symbolic systems approach arose in the early 1980s.

What is (or was) expert systems?

In most fields, knowledge gleaned from training and experience distinguishes experts from amateurs. This seemingly obvious observation was the root of a significant shift of focus in the history of AI. When the field first emerged in the late 1950s, surprisingly little information, much less knowledge, was available or possible to store in digital form, so research naturally focused on methods of reasoning and logic to achieve its goals. But around 1980, a new class of systems, called at the time "expert systems" or "knowledge systems," arose. The idea was to capture and duplicate scarce human expertise in a computable form, in the hope of making this capability available more widely and inexpensively. For reasons I will explain, the field is no longer an active area of research, at least in its original form.

Typically, expert systems were highly specialized or, in the jargon of the time, "domain specific." You might wonder why any program that performs a sufficiently sophisticated task is not considered an expert system, or at least wasn't back when the term was popularized. The main difference is in how the expertise is represented. In contrast to the procedural method of computer programming common at the time (and still today), where a problem is broken down into a series of sequential steps, expert systems instead employed a different approach, a natural application of the symbolic systems concept. These computer programs deconstructed tasks requiring expertise into two components: the "knowledge base"—a collection of facts, rules, and relationships about a specific domain of interest represented in symbolic form—and a general-purpose "inference engine" that described how to manipulate and combine these symbols. Representing the facts and rules explicitly had the advantage that the systems could be more easily modified as new facts or knowledge were incorporated. In particular, the people programming expert systems—who became known as "knowledge engineers"—could create these systems by interviewing practitioners and incrementally incorporating their expertise into computer programs, whose performance could then be tested, evaluated, and improved accordingly. The common approach to programming required the programmer him- or herself to be an expert in the domain, not to mention be readily available to make changes, both obvious practical impediments. By contrast, the concept behind expert systems was to represent the knowledge of the domain explicitly, making it available for inspection and modification. This approach also allowed programs to be more fault tolerant, that is, they tended to be more forgiving of programming mistakes. Equally important, this structure provided a convenient framework for the program to "explain" its reasoning.

As an interesting historical aside, the idea of capturing expertise in "if-then" rules dates back at least to the seventeenth century BCE, when an ancient Egyptian papyrus scroll codified the knowledge of surgeons in this form. In true Indiana Jones style, the document was found and purchased by collector and dealer Edwin Smith from a Luxor curio shop in 1862 but lay unnoticed until it came to the attention of archeologist J. H. Breasted of the

Oriental Institute of the University of Chicago, who translated it into English from the original hieroglyphics in 1930.[17]

A number of companies in the early 1980s were created, mainly by academics and researchers in AI, to sell expert systems products and services. These startups typically offered software packages called "inference engines" and related knowledge engineering consulting services to commercial and governmental organizations wishing to capture and better utilize the capabilities of their own experts.[18] Excitement about this opportunity attracted the attention of venture capital and the press, driving something of a boom and bust not unlike the later investment bubble in Internet companies.

A widely used textbook at the time classified these systems, somewhat imperfectly, into ten categories: interpretation, prediction, diagnosis, design, planning, monitoring, debugging, repair, instruction, and control.[19] But as a practical matter, practitioners in this field often found the tools and frameworks they used lacked sufficient expressive power to capture the breadth of expert knowledge and behavior required to achieve sufficient performance, and so resorted to supplementing their general tools with specialized, handcrafted components, reducing the practical value of their systems.

Expert systems still exist today and indeed are in wide use. The Blaze Advisor business rules management system from FICO is a prominent example. This same company offers widely used rule-based expert systems for credit scoring and analysis.[20]

Today, expert systems are no longer considered an active area of research within AI, much less an investment opportunity, for a number of reasons. Foremost among them is that dramatic increases in computer power, storage, and networking have led to an explosion of data in readily accessible electronic form, which opened the door to a completely different approach to incorporating expertise into computer programs—one that eliminated the need to painstakingly encode the knowledge and skills of a human practitioner by hand.

What is planning?

The symbol system approach is by no means dead. It is alive and well, most prominently in a subfield of AI called "planning," which is concerned with developing techniques to address problems that require formulating a series of steps to accomplish some desired goal. Examples include giving driving directions, playing games, packing odd-sized boxes into a truck, proving mathematical theorems, analyzing legal contracts and regulations, cooking recipes, laying out transistors on computer chips, assembling equipment, describing regulations and rules in computable form, and controlling air traffic.

The common element of these challenges is that there is usually a known initial state, one or more desired final states, a specific set of operations or "moves" available to proceed from initial to final state(s), and some measure of the value of a solution, such as minimizing the number of steps required. In other words, planning systems figure out what to do. While you might suspect that anything goes in solving planning problems, in practice these challenges mostly fall into well-defined classes with characteristic mathematical properties that are amenable to different techniques. You don't approach the problem of finding a needle in a haystack the same way you would try to prove that two triangles are congruent.

With the exception of some probabilistic techniques, most planning systems engage in symbolic inference enhanced with what's called heuristic reasoning. Heuristic reasoning tackles a common, if not universal, problem plaguing the symbolic systems approach—that the number of possible sequences of steps can be very large (called a "combinatorial explosion"), so you can't simply examine all options, as discussed in chapter 1 with respect to the game of chess. Heuristics attempt to reduce the so-called search space to manageable dimensions using a variety of approaches, some of which are guaranteed to reach a proper solution (if it exists), while others run the risk of failing to find a solution, or at least not the best solution ("admissible" versus "inadmissible" heuristics, respectively). For example, if you were trying to climb to the top of a mountain, a pretty good heuristic is to make sure each step you take is uphill—but of course this works only if the hill is a smooth slope upward, never taking a dip. More technically, this incremental approach is called a greedy heuristic (always select the step that gives you the most immediate gain), and works reliably only when domains meet certain criteria for consistency (specifically, if they are monotonic with respect to progress toward the goal).

Planning systems employ a variety of strategies. Some start with the goal and reason backward, in an attempt to find the initial conditions that will get there. For instance, if you have several errands to run but want to be sure to get home in time for dinner at six, you might work backward in time, subtracting how long each stop is going to take you, to figure out when you have to leave. Others reason forward, from hypotheses to conclusions, or attempt to simplify the task by first solving smaller subproblems, then connecting them together into a comprehensive solution.

One active field of AI research that employs planning techniques is "general game playing." This is exactly what it sounds like. A program is presented with a set of rules for playing a game that it has no previous knowledge of, but is told nothing at all about how to play it well. Then it has to figure out its own playing strategies by reasoning about what's likely to work well. As you may expect, there are regular contests among general-game-playing researchers to see whose programs perform best. Since 2005, a contest among general-game-playing enthusiasts at the annual meeting of the Association for the Advancement of Artificial Intelligence has yielded progressively more capable competitors, often able to beat human players already familiar with the selected games.[21] Other widespread modern applications of planning that use heuristic techniques are the navigation programs that provide you with driving directions and what are called "nonplayer characters" (NPCs) in computer games—those seemingly cunning and wily animated characters that often shoot at or antagonize you.

Planning systems, and more generally the symbol systems approach, are what is somewhat derisively (or affectionately, depending on what flavor of AI you happen to be most fond of) today called "Good Old-Fashioned AI," or GOFAI. In any case, subsequent developments have demonstrated that for all its appeal, the physical symbol system hypothesis is not the only game in town.

What is machine learning?

From its earliest days, AI researchers have recognized that the ability to learn is an important aspect of human intelligence. The question is how do people learn? And can we program computers to learn the same way?

Learning is not inconsistent with the physical symbol system hypothesis; it's just not obvious a priori how it fits in. Typically, in an AI application following the symbol systems approach, the learning (if any) is done up front, to help develop the symbols and rules that are ultimately packaged up and used for the intended application. But just as the role of knowledge may have been underappreciated in the earliest AI systems, the importance and value of learning—not only in advance but as an ongoing part of solving many problems of practical interest—may not have received the attention it deserved.

Learning presumably comes mainly from experience, practice, or training, not solely from reasoning, though this can certainly be helpful. To say that something is learned implies that it is more than just captured and stored, as data is in a database—it must be represented in some way that it can be put to use. As a general description, computer programs that learn extract patterns from data. That data may take a seemingly infinite variety of forms—video taken from a moving car, reports of emergency room visits, surface temperatures in the Arctic, Facebook likes, ant trails, recordings of human speech, clicks on online ads, birth records from the Middle Ages, sonar soundings, credit card transactions, the dimming of distant stars when transited by orbiting planets, stock trades, phone calls, ticket purchases, transcripts of legal proceedings, tweets (from both Twitter and birds)—just about anything that can be captured, quantified, or represented in digital form.

People have been collecting and analyzing data for a long time, of course, as anyone who has taken a statistics class well knows. So what's new and different? The vast scale and some of the novel computational techniques that seem to mimic certain aspects of the human brain, suggesting that we may be tantalizingly close to discovering at least some of the hidden secrets of how the mind works. The new data-centric approach to AI goes by several names, most commonly "machine learning," though you may have heard it referred to in the press as "big data" or as "neural networks"—a specific approach to machine learning (but not the only one).

What are artificial neural networks?

To get a feel for what is so innovative about modern machine learning techniques, it is helpful to understand the neural network approach in a bit of detail. An artificial neural network is a computer program inspired by certain presumed organizational principles of a real neural network (such as your brain). The relationship between artificial neural networks and real ones is mostly aspirational. Some researchers in the field of computational neuroscience are explicitly attempting to understand the actual structure of brains and simulate these in a computer, with the goal of understanding how real brains work. Other, more mainstream AI researchers don't really care whether their programs mimic brains, as long as they solve practical problems of interest.

Now the interesting thing is that we know a lot about the structure of the brain at the detail level—that it is composed of a mostly homogeneous mass of cells called neurons, which interconnect with each other at "synapses" to send and receive electrical or chemical signals. When these signals exceed a certain level or form a certain pattern, a neuron "fires," meaning that it in turn signals other neurons that it is connected to. And we know a fair amount about the gross structure of the brain—which layers and regions are typically involved in various activities, such as seeing, getting hungry, doing arithmetic, adjusting your heart rate, recognizing faces, and wiggling your big toe. But surprisingly little is understood about the intermediate structure—how the neurons are connected to perform these tasks. In other words, we don't know much about how the brain is wired (metaphorically speaking). And of course this is precisely the area of interest to AI researchers building artificial neural networks. They simulate the behavior of neurons as individual elements in their programs, then develop techniques for connecting them up and studying the results—what they can do, how quickly, and so on.

Neurons in an artificial neural network are commonly organized into a series of layers. The neurons at each level are connected only to those at the level above and below them in the hierarchy, and the interconnections are usually modeled as numeric weights, with (for instance) 0 representing "not connected" and 1 representing "strongly connected." The lowest level actually receives input from outside the network—for instance, each low-level neuron might process information about a specific dot (pixel) from a camera. The neurons at higher levels—in what are called the "hidden layers"—receive input only from neurons below them. The entire structure is then presented with examples, such as pictures of cats, and the weights are propagated up (and often back down) the hierarchy until it is "tuned" to recognize cats—which is indicated by a particular neuron (or pattern of neurons) firing, usually at the highest level.

You might think that you train an artificial neural network to recognize a cat by showing it pictures with and without cats, indicating which contain cats. You can do it this way, and indeed this is called "supervised learning." But one of the remarkable things about artificial neural networks is that it's actually possible to skip both of these steps. You can present the network only with pictures that contain cats, and you don't have to tell it anything; this is called "unsupervised learning." How can it possibly learn what a cat is, knowing nothing whatsoever about the world, much less about cats? Cat pictures, by themselves, contain patterns—what you recognize as cat faces, whiskers, paws, and so on, in a seemingly endless variety of poses, colors, and angles. But what an artificial neural network actually detects is incredibly sophisticated and complex correlations between the images—regardless of whether they are rotated, stretched, partially obscured, or the like. After training on perhaps millions and millions of images, it develops the ability to detect similar patterns in pictures not presented to it previously. In other words, it learns to identify pictures of cats all by itself.[22] Whether this has anything to do with how we learn to recognize cats is an open question, but what's not open to dispute is that it works, and it works quite well. The most recent crop of such systems can actually outperform humans at many recognition tasks.[23]

To give you an intuitive feel for what's going on here, imagine that you leave a six-string guitar sitting in a room while you play a bunch of loud music in the key of F sharp. As you might expect, the strings would vibrate sympathetically. Then you slowly tighten and/or loosen the tuning peg for each string in turn, while measuring exactly how much that string is vibrating, and leave it adjusted in the position where it vibrates the most before going on to the next. This is a laborious process because, of course, each string responds not only to the sounds in the room but also to the vibration of the other strings. So you have to iterate through the process a large number of times before things start to settle down, meaning that turning any of the tuning pegs only dampens the vibration of that string. Next you play a selection of music in a variety of keys, measuring how much the strings are vibrating. What you are likely to notice is that the vibration is the strongest when you play songs in F sharp and weaker for songs in other keys. Congratulations—you've just built an F sharp key recognizer using an automated process, requiring no knowledge of music or what it "means" to play in F sharp versus D flat or any other key.

Now you decide that while this process worked, it took way too long. So the next time you try it, to speed things up, you move the pegs in larger (or smaller) increments, start them in different positions (that is, with nonstandard guitar tuning), or vary the order in which you adjust each string. You might find that certain starting positions, for instance, don't work at all— you never get the whole system vibrating strongly enough to identify music in F sharp, or you wind up going in circles, repeatedly tightening and loosening the same strings. This is analogous to much of research in artificial neural networks—a great deal of effort is going into figuring out how to set up initial conditions, propagate connection weights, and get them to converge to the best or an acceptable solution in a reasonable amount of time. The nature of current work in the field is reminiscent of research in power electrics around the turn of the last century—dominated by empirical attempts to build systems, then test them—until a more formal analytic methodology was developed. Hopefully, such a framework will emerge for machine learning as well.

In summary, you can think of artificial neural networks as constructions that resonate with arbitrarily complex patterns present in their inputs. They are mirrors of their experience. In this sense, they don't "learn how to do things" in the common sense of the phrase—developing a principled understanding of the underlying relationships and properties of their world.

Instead, they are incredibly skilled mimics, finding correlations and responding to novel inputs as if to say, "This reminds me of . . . ," and in doing so imitate successful strategies gleaned from a large collection of examples. An open philosophical question is whether this approach is equivalent to understanding causation. Are we really doing the same thing, or is there something more to the way humans learn and interact with the world? And if the end result—the behavior—is the same, does any such distinction matter?

How did machine learning arise?

You might wonder when machine learning, a radically different approach to AI, was invented, given that it wasn't taken seriously by leaders in the field until well into the late 1980s and early 1990s. It actually dates back to at least 1943, when Warren McCulloch and Walter Pitts, then at the University of Chicago, observed that a network of brain neurons could be modeled by, of all things, logical expressions. In short, they recognized that despite the fact that brains are soft, wet, gelatinous masses, the signaling in the brain is digital. Indeed it appears to be binary. This is another example of the role that mathematical formalization can play in propelling science forward, as I discussed in chapter 1. Since programmable computers were largely unknown when McCulloch and Pitts made this important observation, or at least were mostly under development in secret government projects for use in war, using their work as the basis for computer programs wasn't foremost in their minds. That said, they recognized the potential computational implications: "Specification of the nervous net provides the law of necessary connection whereby one can compute from the description of any state that of the succeeding state."[24] Indeed, they seemed most excited by the possibility that modeling the brain mathematically could lead to progress in treating psychiatric disorders, which was natural since McCulloch, by far the senior member of the team, was an MD and psychologist.

Several subsequent researchers continued this early work, most notably Frank Rosenblatt of Cornell (supported by grants from the U.S. Navy), who rebranded his own implementation of an artificial neuron as a "perceptron," garnering considerable press attention. The *New York Times*, in a remarkable example of gullible reporting, published an article in 1958 entitled "New Navy Device Learns by Doing: Psychologist Shows Embryo of Computer Designed to Read and Grow Wiser," in which it proclaimed, "The Navy revealed the embryo of an electronic computer today that it expects will be able to walk, talk, see, write, reproduce itself and be conscious of its existence.... [It] is expected to be finished in about a year at a cost of $100,000.... Later Perceptrons will be able to recognize people and call out their names and instantly translate speech in one language to speech or writing in another language." Rosenblatt predicted in the article that "perceptrons might be fired to the planets as mechanical space explorers ... the machine would be the first device to think as the human brain ... in principle it would be possible to build brains that could reproduce themselves on an assembly line and which would be conscious of their existence." This might seem a bit optimistic given that his demonstration included only four hundred photocells (four hundred pixel images) connected to a thousand perceptrons which, after fifty trials were able to tell the difference between "two cards, one with squares marked on the left side and the other with squares on the right side."[25] On the other hand, many of his wilder prophecies have now become reality, though more than fifty years later than he predicted.

Rosenblatt's work was well known to at least some of the participants at the Dartmouth conference. He had attended the Bronx High School of Science with Marvin Minsky (they were one year apart).[26] They were later to become sparring debaters in many forums, promoting their respectively favored approaches to AI, until in 1969 Minsky, along with his colleague Seymour Papert at MIT, published a book called *Perceptrons*, in which he went to pains to discredit, rather unfairly, a simplified version of Rosenblatt's work.[27] Rosenblatt was unable to mount a proper defense, as he died in a boating accident in 1971 at the age of forty-one.[28] Minsky and Papert's book proved highly influential, effectively foreclosing funding and research on perceptrons and artificial neural networks in general for more than a decade.

Addressing the very oversimplification that Minsky and Papert exploited—that the network has at most two layers—was in part responsible for a revival of interest in the field in the mid-1980s. Indeed, the area of "deep learning"—a major current focus in machine learning—refers to the use of artificial neural networks that have many internal layers (referred to as hidden layers). But the main driver of renewed interest in the field was the growing availability of example data in computer-readable form, not to mention that computers were improving at a blistering pace in terms of both storage and processing capacity. In particular, a new class of powerful parallel processing supercomputers called connection machines could simulate the behavior of multiple artificial neurons at the same time.[29]

Despite the promise of these novel machines, they were ultimately overtaken by standard nonparallel commercial processors because the economics of mass production accelerated their development faster than such specialized machines. The same fate was to befall another related computer engineering development at the time—machines designed specifically to process McCarthy's AI language LISP. A new attempt to develop processors targeted to artificial neural networks is currently under way, most notably at IBM.[30] Its latest effort is a 5.4-billion-transistor chip with 4,096 neurosynaptic cores that integrates 1 million neurons and 256 million synapses. Each chip supports a thousand times as many artificial neurons as Rosenblatt's implementations and they can be tiled and stacked in two dimensions, not to mention they probably operate at least 1 million times faster. In a slightly disquieting echo of Rosenblatt's earlier enthusiasm, Dharmendra Modha, a leader of the project at IBM, has been quoted as saying, "It's a new landmark of the brain-inspired computers ... [it] approximate[s] the structure and function of the brain in silicon."[31] Time will tell if this proves to be the computer architecture of the future or simply another misguided attempt to build computers tailored for a specialized class of applications.

While machine learning systems are currently experiencing a boom in commercial investment and being applied to an incredible variety of problems with significant success, perhaps the most remarkable application is some recent work in which the techniques are used not to simulate the brain but to reverse engineer it. A group of scientists led by Jack Gallant at the Henry H. Wheeler Jr. Brain Imaging Center of the University of California at Berkeley is succeeding in using machine learning techniques to read minds.[32] Really. The researchers train a machine learning system to look for patterns from an array of brain sensors while they show test subjects pictures of various objects, like scissors, bottles, or shoes. Then they put a new subject into the test rig and show him or her a picture. Once trained, their program can correctly identify what the subject is looking at with significant accuracy.

There are two promising aspects of this research. First, the techniques currently used to measure brain activity are quite crude, mainly blood flow occurring in cubic brain segments three millimeters on a side (called "voxels"), the modern equivalent of Rosenblatt's low-resolution twenty-by-twenty grid of photocells. As brain activity measurement instruments become more sensitive and detailed, potentially even detecting the firing of individual neurons, the quality of the interpretations is likely to improve dramatically. Second, the results are not specific to a particular person—the system can train on one set of test subjects, then use those results to interpret what a different subject is looking at with high accuracy. This means that at least to the level of detail researchers are currently studying, human brains are not as idiosyncratic as one might suppose.

Already there are efforts to commercialize some of these concepts—for example, the company No Lie MRI purports to use MRI studies to determine whether an individual is being truthful or not (though it is not clear to what degree the company is employing machine learning techniques).[33]

Unless (or until) fundamental limitations emerge, this work opens up the real prospect of integrating our own brains with the electronic world—in other words, communicating with and controlling computers, machines, and robots simply with our minds, just as we do our own bodies. It also raises the scary prospect that our own thoughts may no longer be entirely private.

Which approach is better, symbolic reasoning or machine learning?

Though most researchers are focused exclusively on one or the other of these two approaches, there's no reason in principle that they can't both be profitably integrated into a single design. Indeed, there is considerable effort in this direction and conferences devoted to it.[34]

But the plain fact is that these approaches have different strengths and weaknesses. In general, symbolic reasoning is more appropriate for problems that require abstract reasoning, while machine learning is better for situations that require sensory perception or extracting patterns from noisy data. For instance, suppose you want to build a robot that can ride a bike (that is, one that can control the pedals and handlebars, and is able to balance). Representing this problem in symbolic terms may be possible, but imagine trying to interview a human expert in an effort to build an expert system to do this. There certainly are experts at riding bikes, but the nature of their expertise simply doesn't lend itself to description in words. Clearly, knowledge and expertise can take forms that resist codification into human language or any explicitly symbolic form.

By contrast, using machine learning techniques, this problem is a ride in the park, so to speak. For a single example, a recent research project by some graduate students at the Georgia Institute of Technology accomplished this task using neural network techniques; the system succeeded in learning stunts such as wheelies, the "bunny hop," front wheel pivot, and back hop (this particular system learns in a simulator, not on an actual bicycle).[35]

But there are other issues for which machine learning techniques aren't well suited. To state the obvious, machine learning is not useful for problems where there's no data, just some initial conditions, a bunch of constraints, and one shot to get it right. For example, mistakes made in the design of computer chips can be very expensive and damaging. After Intel was forced to recall its Pentium 5 processor in 1994 due to a bug in certain math functions, interest surged in formal methods for verifying that circuits performed as expected. There are two parts to this problem: first, how to describe in an abstract way the functions of the circuit that you are trying to verify; and second, how to perform the test in a practical amount of time and at an acceptable cost while still guaranteeing that the results are correct. After a decade of work on this problem, a language for specifying the desired behavior was accepted and standardized by the IEEE (Institute for Electrical and Electronic Engineers) in 2005, followed by a variety of commercial and proprietary programs to perform the actual verification.[36] But the field of AI suffers from an unusual deficiency—once a particular problem is considered solved, it often is no longer considered AI. So "formal verification" and "model checking," at least as applied to computer hardware, are now independent fields, though they trace their intellectual roots back to early theorem provers like that of Newell and Simon.

That said, many problems that you might think of as requiring logic and reasoning are surprisingly amenable to machine learning techniques. For instance, recent work at MIT and the University of Washington can solve typical high school–level algebraic word problems with a 70 percent success rate—not by reasoning, but by learning from pairs of word problems and their associated equations (solutions) gleaned from algebra.com, a homework help website. After training on the dataset, the program is able to solve problems like the following: "An amusement park sells 2 kinds of tickets. Tickets for children cost $1.50. Adult tickets cost $4. On a certain day, 278 people entered the park. On that same day the admission fees collected totaled $792. How many children were admitted on that day? How many adults were admitted?"[37] Recent results in chess-playing programs are equally surprising. Instead of incorporating specialized knowledge and strategies about how to play the game, as most chess-playing programmers do, a group of researchers used a technique called "genetic programming" to evolve a program that plays at an expert level, giving it access only to a database of human grandmaster games.[38] (Genetic programming, a form of machine learning, generates successive generations of candidate solutions, evaluates their relative performance, then carries only the fittest, with some mutations, to the next generation.)

If you were to make a list of human activities that would seem to require insight, creativity, intelligence, and logic, surely solving a *New York Times* crossword puzzle would be on it. But a program playfully called Dr.Fill (no space, that's not a typo) performs this task at an expert level and in seconds—not by incorporating a deep understanding of the world but by applying what's called "constraint satisfaction" and statistical machine learning techniques to a library of over forty-seven thousand puzzles and clues.[39] For example, given the clue "Jacket material, for short?" (three letters), it can enter "bio" as the correct answer. Dr.Fill is a rare example of a program that combines both symbolic reasoning and machine learning techniques to solve a complex, real-world problem.

In short, if you have to stare at a problem and think about it, a symbolic reasoning approach is probably more appropriate. If you have to look at lots of examples or play around with the issue to get a "feel" for it, machine learning is likely to be more effective. So why did the focus of work shift from the former to the latter?

In the early days of AI, the available computers were simply not powerful enough to machine learn much of interest. They offered only a miniscule fraction of the processing speed of today's computers and sported an equally vanishing amount of memory available to store data. But most important, there simply weren't many sources of machine-readable data available to learn from. Most communication was on paper and available only at specific locations—as anyone who has tried to get their mother's birth certificate can attest. For real-time learning, the data from sensors was equally primitive or available only in an analog form that resisted processing digitally. So four trends—improvements in computing speed and memory, the transition from physically to electronically stored data, easier access (mainly due to the Internet), and low-cost high-resolution digital sensors—were prime drivers in the refocusing of effort from symbolic reasoning to machine learning.

What are some of the most important historical milestones in AI?

This question can be answered from several perspectives. Certainly, there have been technical and scientific breakthroughs that are significant intellectual achievements underlying many of the great advances in the field, but these are beyond our current scope.[40] There are also many highly successful applications with great impact on society that are secret, proprietary, or otherwise hidden from view. Examples include programs that scan our communications (for better or for worse), trade securities, detect cyber attacks, review our credit card transactions for fraud, and no doubt many others. But there are some notable accomplishments that break through to the popular press that you may already be familiar with. While I have attempted to select examples in this book that will augment your understanding of the field as opposed to repeat what you already know, I would be remiss in not mentioning a few more visible results.

Probably the first objective and easily comprehensible milestone to capture the public's imagination was the program Deep Blue, which beat Garry Kasparov, then the world chess champion, in a six-game tournament in 1997.[41] The program, developed by some former Carnegie Mellon University researchers hired by IBM to continue their work, was named after the company's corporate color and nickname—Big Blue. The match was a nail-biter —Deep Blue triumphed only in the final game. Adding to the drama, Kasparov, a child prodigy considered possibly the greatest chess player of all time (and apparently a bit of a prima donna at the age of thirty-four), promptly accused IBM of cheating, based mainly on his conviction that a machine could never have formulated such brilliant strategies.

In any case, this victory, after decades of missed predictions by overly optimistic prognosticators, received widespread attention and sparked endless debates about what it "meant" for human supremacy over machines. Chess had long been held out as a bastion of intellectual achievement likely to resist any attempt at automation. But like most if not all such encroachments by technology into formerly exclusively human domains, the accomplishment was soon accepted as routine rather than a call to arms that mechanical minds were approaching from all directions to take over the world. Those downplaying the import of the victory mostly focused on the role of the specially designed supercomputer used for the task rather than the sophisticated programming techniques developed by the team, which suited IBM just fine, since the company was in the business of selling the latest and greatest hardware. Explanations of the programming techniques used also helped to demystify this fear: if you can see the emperor's naked body, perhaps he's not so superhuman after all. Today, expert-level computer chess-playing programs are commonplace and so powerful that they are no longer routinely pitted against human players. Instead, numerous computer-only championship contests are held annually, for instance, by the International Computer Games Association.[42] By 2009, chess programs capable of grandmaster-level play could be run on a garden-variety smartphone.[43]

With computer chess now regarded as a "solved problem," attention moved on to a completely different sort of challenge: driving a car without human intervention. The main technological barrier is not control of the car—most modern vehicles already interpose electronics between the driver and the controls—but rather the ability to sense the environment in sufficient detail and respond quickly enough. An emerging technology call LIDAR (for light/laser detection and ranging), mainly used for military mapping and targeting, proved just the ticket for sensing, but interpreting the results was another matter. Integrating the stream of data into features and obstructions of interest—such as trees, cars, people, and bicycles—required significant advances in the state of the art of computer vision (which I will describe in chapter 3).

To accelerate progress on this problem, DARPA, charged with promoting U.S. technological superiority, established the Grand Challenge, with a prize of $1 million to go to the first vehicle to finish a prearranged 150-mile route through rugged terrain. The first contest was held in 2004 in the Mojave Desert, but none of the entrants made it further than about 7 miles. Undaunted, DARPA scheduled a second contest for 2005, and despite the previous year's lackluster performance, twenty-three teams entered the race. This time, the results were entirely different: five entrants completed the challenge. Taking the lead was a team from Stanford University, which finished the run in just under seven hours, with two teams from Carnegie Mellon University close behind. It was a harrowing course, traversing Beer Bottle Pass, a narrow, winding mountain road with a steep drop on one side, and passing through three narrow tunnels.[44] But DARPA wasn't quite satisfied. It scheduled a third contest in 2007, called the Urban Challenge, to navigate a sixty-mile course on streets—complete with street signs, signals, and cross traffic. (It was held on a closed military base in Southern California.) This time, a team from Carnegie Mellon University bested the previous winner from Stanford, averaging fourteen miles per hour.[45]

The rest, as they say, is history. Sebastian Thrun, leader of the Stanford team and then director of the Stanford AI Lab, joined Google Research to start a project to develop a practical autonomous vehicle, a program soon emulated by major automobile manufacturers around the world. Today, the technology has found its way into numerous vehicles but, as of this writing, concerns about public acceptance and potential liability have prevented the car companies from permitting fully hands-off driving by consumers, a restriction likely to be progressively relaxed in the coming years.[46]

But perhaps the most impressive and best-known public win for AI was literally a win—on the TV quiz show *Jeopardy*. As the story is told, an IBM research manager named Charles Lickel, at dinner with colleagues in 2004, noticed that many of the patrons had turned their attention to the television, which showed *Jeopardy* champion Ken Jennings in the middle of his record-setting seventy-four game winning streak. Recognizing a potential follow-on to IBM's success with Deep Blue, he suggested to his companions that they try their hand at building a computer program to play the game. After seven years of development by a team of fifteen people and extensive negotiations with the production staff of the show, IBM's program—named Watson after the company's founder—beat Ken Jennings and Brad Rutter (another champion) on January 14, 2011. (The show was broadcast in February.) Watson's score, which is measured in dollars, was $35,734, compared to Rutter at $10,400 and Jennings at $4,800.[47] To accomplish this feat, Watson used a database of 200 million pages of facts and figures, including the full text of Wikipedia, occupying four terabytes of storage. By 2015, you could buy an external hard drive to connect to your home computer sufficient to hold this information for a mere $120.

Remarkable as this accomplishment was, there was a trick to Watson's triumph. It turns out that most *Jeopardy* champions know the answer to most clues most of the time; it just may take them some time to figure it out. The real key to winning is to ring in more quickly than the other contestants after the clue is read. In contrast to human players, Watson didn't "read" the clue off the game board—it was transmitted electronically at the start. While the other contestants took several seconds to scan the clue and decide whether or not to ring in, Watson could use that time to search for an answer. More important, it could ring in a few short milliseconds after the host finished reading the clue out loud, far faster than a human could press a button. So while the program's ability to respond to these subtle and often baffling clues was certainly exceptional, its natural speed advantages as a machine were a major factor in its success.

But IBM's business isn't winning contests—it's selling computers and software. So in 2014 the company announced that it was forming a major business unit to commercialize the technology, investing $1 billion and employing two thousand people to develop the Watson "ecosystem" and foster the development of a wide range of commercial, scientific, and governmental applications based on the technology.[48]

Not to be outdone, a group of researchers at Google's DeepMind division applied their machine learning algorithms to the ancient game of Go, where two opponents attempt to encircle each other by alternately placing white and black stones on a 19 by 19 grid.[49] Go swamps chess with respect to the number of possible moves, making it resistant to solution by many other AI approaches, such as the heuristic search techniques IBM's Deep Blue mainly used to beat Kasparov at chess. The Google program, named AlphaGo, scored a decisive win over Lee Sedol, a top-ranked international Go player, winning 4 out of a 5-game series in South Korea in March of 2016.

The win was certainly a significant technical achievement, but what it means for machine intelligence and its relationship to human intelligence is unclear at best. Fei-Fei Li, Director of the Stanford AI Lab, put this well. She was quoted in the *New York Times* as saying "I'm not surprised at all. How come we are not surprised that a car runs faster than the fastest human?"[50]

Notes

1. J. McCarthy, M. L. Minsky, N. Rochester, and C. E. Shannon, "A Proposal for the Dartmouth Summer Research Project on Artificial Intelligence," 1955, http://www-formal.stanford.edu/jmc/history/dartmouth/dartmouth.html.

2. John McCarthy, June 13, 2000, review of *The Question of Artificial Intelligence* (1961), edited by Brian Bloomfield, on McCarthy's personal website at http://www-formal.stanford.edu/jmc/reviews/bloomfield/bloomfield.html. In the review, McCarthy comments, "As for myself, one of the reasons for inventing the term 'artificial intelligence' was to escape association with 'cybernetics.' Its concentration on analog feedback seemed misguided, and I wished to avoid having either to accept Norbert (not Robert) Wiener as a guru or having to argue with him." I'm indebted to John Markoff of the *New York Times* for bringing this reference to my attention.

3. McCarthy et al., "A Proposal for the Dartmouth Summer Research Project."

4. Ibid.

5. Indeed, hostility toward AI continues to this day. One of the reviewers of the proposal for this book (who nearly prevented its publication) had this to say: "This is yet another representative of the kind of breezy, brash, and cocky work AI enthusiasts have published in the past.... If the author wishes his readers to know 'everything about AI' then he should confine himself to what has been actually achieved, not what he predicts will be achieved.... The AI world is notorious for its bad predictions made about intelligent systems and what they will do.... *I cannot recommend it in its present form.*"

6. Samuel Arthur, "Some Studies in Machine Learning Using the Game of Checkers," *IBM Journal* 3, no 3 (1959): 210–29.

7. Allen Newell and Herbert A. Simon, "The Logic Theory Machine: A Complex Information Processing System," June 15, 1956, report from the Rand Corporation, Santa Monica, CA, http://shelf1. library.cmu.edu/IMLS/MindModels/logictheorymachine.pdf; Alfred North Whitehead and Bertrand Russell, *Principia Mathematica* (Cambridge: Cambridge University Press, 1910).
8. A. Newell and H. A. Simon, "GPS: A Program That Simulates Human Thought," in *Lernende automaten*, ed. H. Billings (Munich: R. Oldenbourg, 1961), 109–24. See also G. Ernst and A. Newell, *GPS: A Case Study in Generality and Problem Solving* (New York: Academic Press, 1969).
9. Hubert L. Dreyfus, "Alchemy and Artificial Intelligence," December 1965, report from the Rand Corporation, P-3244, http://www.rand .org/content/dam/rand/pubs/papers/2006/P3244.pdf.
10. Hubert L. Dreyfus, *What Computers Can't Do: The Limits of Artificial Intelligence* (New York: Harper & Row, 1972), 100.
11. "Shakey," SRI International Artificial Intelligence Center, http:// www.ai.sri.com/shakey/.
12. Terry Winograd, "Procedures as a Representation for Data in a Computer Program for Understanding Natural Language," MIT AI Technical Report 235, February 1971. For an entertaining explanation of how and why Winograd named his program SHRDLU, see http://hci.stanford.edu/winograd/shrdlu/name.html.
13. This snippet of dialog is copied from the Wikipedia page on SHRDLU (http://en.wikipedia.org/wiki/SHRDLU) for convenience, but Winograd's PhD thesis included a number of other examples ("Procedures as a Representation for Data").
14. For an in-depth look at the AI versus HCI threads in the history of the field, see John Markoff, *Machines of Loving Grace: The Quest for Common Ground between Humans and Robots* (New York: Ecco, 2015).
15. Carl Hewitt, "PLANNER: A Language for Proving Theorems," MIT Computer Science and Artificial Intelligence Laboratory (CSAIL) A.I. memo 137 (1967), ftp://publications.ai.mit.edu/ai-publications/pdf/AIM-137.pdf.
16. Allen Newell and Herbert Simon, "Computer Science as Empirical Inquiry: Symbols and Search," 1975 ACM Turing Award Lecture, *Communications of the ACM* 19, no. 3 (1976), https://www.cs.utexas .edu/~kuipers/readings/Newell+Simon-cacm-76.pdf.
17. https://oi.uchicago.edu/research/publications/oip/edwin-smith-surgical-papyrus-volume-1-hieroglyphic-transliteration.

18. I was cofounder of one of these expert systems companies, Teknow-ledge, Inc., which went public in 1984 and remained in active operation through 2005.

19. Frederick Hayes-Roth, Donald Waterman, and Douglas Lenat, *Building Expert Systems* (Boston: Addison-Wesley, 1983), as summarized at http://en.wikipedia.org/wiki/Expert_system.

20. http://www.fico.com/en/latest-thinking/product-sheet/fico-blaze-advisor-business-rules-management-product-sheet.

21. For more information, see the General Game Playing website of Professor Michael Genesereth of Stanford University's Logic Group, http://games.stanford.edu.

22. Quoc V. Le, Marc'Aurelio Ranzato, Rajat Monga, Matthieu Devin, Kai Chen, Greg S. Corrado, Jeffrey Dean, and Andrew Y. Ng, "Building High-Level Features Using Large Scale Unsupervised Learning," (paper presented at the Twenty-Ninth International Conference on Machine Learning, Edinburgh, June 2012), http://research.google .com/archive/unsupervised_icml2012.html.

23. Kaiming He, Xiangyu Zhang, Shaoqing Ren, and Jian Sun, "Delving Deep into Rectifiers: Surpassing Human-Level Performance on ImageNet Classification," February 6, 2015, http://arxiv.org/abs/1502.01852.

24. Warren McCulloch and Walter Pitts, "A Logical Calculus of Ideas Immanent in Nervous Activity," *Bulletin of Mathematical Biophysics* 5, no. 4 (1943): 115–33, (p. 130), http://deeplearning.cs.cmu.edu/pdfs/ McCulloch.and.Pitts.pdf.

25. "New Navy Device Learns by Doing: Psychologist Shows Embryo of Computer Designed to Read and Grow Wiser," *New York Times*, July 8, 1958, http://timesmachine.nytimes.com/timesmachine/1958/ 07/08/83417341.html?pageNumber=25.

26. http://en.wikipedia.org/wiki/Perceptrons_(book).

27. Marvin Minsky and Seymour Papert, *Perceptrons: An Introduction to Computational Geometry*, 2nd ed. (Cambridge, MA: MIT Press, 1972).

28. http://en.wikipedia.org/wiki/Frank_Rosenblatt.

29. For example, see W. Daniel Hillis, *The Connection Machine*, MIT Press Series in Artificial Intelligence (Cambridge, MA: MIT Press, 1986).

30. Paul A. Merolla, John V. Arthur, Rodrigo Alvarez-Icaza, Andrew S. Cassidy, Jun Sawada, Filipp Akopyan, Bryan L. Jackson, Nabil Imam, Chen Guo, Yutaka Nakamura, Bernard Brezzo, Ivan Vo, Steven K. Esser, Rathinakumar Appuswamy, Brian Taba, Arnon Amir, Myron D. Flickner, William P. Risk, Rajit Manohar, and Dharmendra S. Modha, "A Million Spiking-Neuron Integrated Circuit with a

Scalable Communication Network and Interface," *Science*, August 2014, 668–73, http://www.sciencemag.org/content/345/6197/668.

31. Joab Jackson, "IBM's New Brain-Mimicking Chip Could Power the Internet of Things," IDG News Service, August 7, 2014, http://www.pcworld.com/article/2462960/ibms-new-brain-chip-could-power-the-internet-of-things.html.

32. For example, see Kerri Smith, "Brain Decoding: Reading Minds," *Nature*, October 23, 2013, 428–30, http://www.nature.com/polopoly_fs/1.13989!/menu/main/topColumns/topLeftColumn/pdf/502428a.pdf.

33. No Lie MRI: http://www.noliemri.com/index.htm.

34. "Knowledge Representation and Reasoning: Integrating Symbolic and Neural Approaches," AAAI Spring Symposium on KRR, Stanford University, CA, March 23–25, 2015, https://sites.google.com/site/krr2015/. In particular, for an overview of the state of the art among the papers presented at the symposium, see Artur d'Avila Garcez, Tarek R. Besold, Luc de Raedt, Peter Földiak, Pascal Hitzler, Thomas Icard, Kai-Uwe Kühnberger, Luis C. Lamb, Risto Miikkulainen, and Daniel L. Silver, "Neural-Symbolic Learning and Reasoning: Contributions and Challenges," http://www.aaai.org/ocs/index.php/SSS/SSS15/paper/viewFile/10281/10029.

35. Jie Tan, Yuting Gu, Karen Liu, and Greg Turk, "Learning Bicycle Stunts," *ACM Transactions on Graphics* 33, no. 4 (2014), http://www.cc.gatech.edu/~jtan34/project/learningBicycleStunts.html.

36. "IEEE P1850—Standard for PSL—Property Specification Language," December 9, 2007, http://ieeexplore.ieee.org/xpl/freeabs_all.jsp?arnumber=4408637.

37. Nate Kushman, Yoav Artzi, Luke Zettlemoyer, and Regina Barzilay, "Learning to Automatically Solve Algebra Word Problems," in *Proceedings of the 52nd Annual Meeting of the Association for Computational Linguistics*, vol. 1, *Long Papers* (2014), 271–81, http://people.csail.mit.edu/nkushman/papers/acl2014.pdf.

38. Omid E. David, H. Jaap van den Herik, Moshe Koppel, and Nathan S. Netanyahu, "Genetic Algorithms for Evolving Computer Chess Programs," *IEEE Transactions on Evolutionary Computation* 18, no. 5 (2014): 779–89, http://www.genetic-programming.org/hc2014/David-Paper.pdf.

39. Matthew L. Ginsberg, "Dr.Fill: Crosswords and an Implemented Solver for Singly Weighted CSPs," *Journal of Artificial Intelligence Research* 42 (2011): 851–86.

40. For an excellent and meticulous history of the field, see Nils J. Nilsson, *The Quest for Artificial Intelligence* (Cambridge: Cambridge University Press, 2009).

41. Feng-hsiung Hsu, *Behind Deep Blue: Building the Computer That Defeated the World Chess Champion* (Princeton, NJ: Princeton University Press, 2002).

42. International Computer Games Association, http://icga.leidenuniv.nl.

43. http://en.wikipedia.org/wiki/Computer_chess.

44. Steve Russell, "DARPA Grand Challenge Winner: Stanley the Robot!" *Popular Mechanics*, January 8, 2006, http://www.popular-mechanics.com/technology/robots/a393/2169012/.

45. John Markoff, "Crashes and Traffic Jams in Military Test of Robotic Vehicles," *New York Times*, November 5, 2007, http://www.nytimes.com/2007/11/05/technology/05robot.html.

46. That said, I recently took a test drive in a commercially available car (Tesla Model S) that offers autonomous highway driving. No doubt by the time you read this the experience will be commonplace.

47. http://en.wikipedia.org/wiki/Watson_(computer).

48. "IBM Watson Group Unveils Cloud-Delivered Watson Services to Transform Industrial R&D, Visualize Big Data Insights and Fuel Analytics Exploration," IBM press release, January 9, 2014, http://www-03.ibm.com/press/us/en/pressrelease/42869.wss.

49. For more information, see the American Go Association, http://www.usgo.org/what-go.

50. Choe Sang-Hun and John Markoff, "Master of Go Board Game Is Walloped by Google Computer Program," *New York Times*, March 9, 2016.

3

FRONTIERS OF ARTIFICIAL INTELLIGENCE

What are the main areas of research and development in AI?

Work in artificial intelligence is generally divided into a number of subfields that address common, though difficult, practical problems or require different tools or skills. Some of the more prominent are robotics, computer vision, speech recognition, and natural language processing. A brief explanation of each follows.

What is robotics?

Robotics should require little description—it involves building machines that are capable of performing physical tasks. Most people think of robots as mimicking human form, but of course that's not necessary. Much ongoing work seeks to develop lighter-weight, more flexible, stronger materials and methods of control as well as novel designs (often inspired by nature), but what really distinguishes robotic research in AI from more pedestrian mechanical automation is the attempt to build devices that are capable of more general classes of tasks. For instance, all sorts of special-purpose machines exist that pack specific foods and products into shipping cartons and containers. But creating a single device capable of handling a wide variety of shapes, sizes, weights, and fragility remains a challenge at the forefront of AI.[1] The main issue here is adapting to changing or chaotic environments as they continually shift. The signature accomplishment of robotics research in this regard is the autonomous vehicle, which navigates roads and negotiates spaces in concert with human-controlled vehicles, bicycles, and pedestrians, despite all the attendant novelty and unpredictability.

AI technology opens whole new vistas of economic opportunity by enabling robots to work where people can't. Robots are of great value for all sorts of tasks that are too dangerous or costly for people to do. These might be mining or farming the sea bottom, eliminating agricultural pests by targeting them with insect-specific mechanical predators, or cleaning up industrial accidents.

One obvious such area is exploration of space. In 1993, NASA sent the space shuttle with seven people on board on a mission to repair the Hubble space station; the objective was to perform an exceptionally precise operation to correct the space telescope's optics. This was the first of five manned Hubble maintenance missions.[2] In 2004, serious consideration was given to using a two-armed Canadian robot called Dextre instead of astronauts for the final mission, but it was judged too risky given the state of the art at the time.[3] Nonetheless, robotic devices are likely to be much more practical for the sorts of tasks we are likely to want to perform off the earth in the near future, such as analyzing geological samples, searching for biological life, mining asteroids, and diverting astronomical bodies whose paths threaten earth. The NASA Mars rovers—*Opportunity* and *Curiosity*—are prime examples of this approach, though the degree to which they rely on AI technology is less clear.[4]

Closer to home, the most recent DARPA robotics challenge was motivated by the difficulty of getting human personnel into the Fukushima nuclear plants following their meltdown.[5] Teams competed to have their robots perform a variety of common tasks such as driving a utility vehicle, opening a door, locating and closing a valve, and connecting a fire hose to a standpipe.

Eldercare is another area of active robotic research, motivated by the demographically driven aging of many Western societies, notably in Japan. There are a number of efforts under way to offer robotic assistance to the infirm, aged, and incapacitated, but the most practical are focused on specific tasks, like ensuring that patients take their medication or help them move from bed to a wheelchair.[6] Despite what you see in movies such as *Robot & Frank*, home robots are a very long way from providing the sort of general assistance that a human caregiver typically provides.[7]

A separate class of assistive robots offers psychological as opposed to physical comfort. For instance, the therapeutic robot Paro provides the benefits of "animal therapy" to cognitively impaired patients.[8] Mimicking the appearance of a furry baby seal, it responds to holding, petting, and so on. Paro has been shown to improve socialization, increase relaxation, and boost motivation. However, these artificially "emotional" robots are not without controversy. MIT professor Sherry Turkle, who studies the social effects of technology, warns that mechanical devices that encourage emotional bonding are inherently deceptive and potentially harmful to human relationships.[9]

Then there are robots for entertainment. These usually take anthropomorphic forms like the preprogrammed animatronic figures common in theme parks such as Disneyland but are considerably more flexible and interactive. Pepper, from Alderbaran Robotics and SoftBank Mobile, tries to read your intentions and respond appropriately.[10] It is currently used to greet visitors to SoftBank stores in Japan, where it can answer limited questions about products and services, but its primary value is to engage and delight customers. There have also been many generations of interactive toy robots. From Hasbro's Furby to Sony's robotic dog AIBO (recently withdrawn from production), these gadgets are intended to enchant children and charm adults with increasing sophistication and responsiveness.[11]

The dream of a personal mechanical servant is as old as robotics itself, but the popular image of a humanoid maid, in the style of Rosie on the classic animated TV show *The Jetsons*, remains a distant dream. The actual state of the art is exemplified by the Roomba autonomous vacuum cleaner (from iRobot), which scurries about floors and carpets, avoids steps, docks itself into its charging station when low on power, and generally tries to stay out of your way while doing its work. The latest version (as of this writing) is the Roomba 980, which incrementally builds a map of your home to ensure that it thoroughly cleans your entire space, whereas previous versions simply scurried around randomly.[12]

One of the most exciting recent developments in the field is known as "swarm robotics." Large collections of relatively simple uniform robots are programmed with rules, and when these are applied in aggregate to the entire group, the robots exhibit complex behavior, called "emergent behavior." This same effect is observed in anthills and beehives, whose members as communities solve problems that are far beyond the comprehension or capabilities of any individual. While swarm robots could be any size, much research is focused on small (insect-sized) or microscopic ("nanorobotic") scales. Collections of these devices can work together to perform some task, for instance, locating people trapped in collapsed buildings or detecting toxic spills. They typically coordinate by forming ad hoc networks or communicating peer to peer with nearby units.

It's difficult to exaggerate the potential benefits and dangers of this technology. On the positive side, it could facilitate tremendous medical advances, such as performing noninvasive surgical procedures from inside the body. Imagine a syringe full of robots the size of T-cells that mimic the function of the immune system, able to seek and attack blood-borne cancers. Or a shoebox full of robots the size of cockroaches that scurry around collecting dust from floors and walls, stuffing their bounty into a small bag for easy disposal. Imagine releasing thousands of mole-sized robots to explore for minerals underground, followed by tiny robotic miners.

But there are also significant dangers. The same technology that might cure blood-borne cancers can be used to kill you, or perhaps even to control you.[13] Anyone who has tried to eliminate ants from the kitchen knows how difficult it can be to prevent an invasion by a tiny, organized army. The potential military or terrorist applications of swarm robotics are truly too horrific to contemplate.

Related research on multi-robot collaboration, typically at larger scales, aims to coordinate the activity of groups of robots dynamically, usually from some centralized computing resource. For instance, Kiva Systems, a warehouse management robotics company purchased by Amazon in 2012, coordinates the actions of a fleet of robots to bring products from shelves to (human) order packers.[14] To inspire and promote research on multi-robot systems, a RoboCup competition is staged annually, wherein teams compete to win a robotic soccer contest (the formal name is the Robot Soccer World Cup).[15]

Military applications are too numerous, and perhaps dangerous, to mention. While the popular imagination conjures up visions of *Terminator*-style robotic soldiers running around a theater of battle bearing arms, the truth is very different. Military robots will not be designed to *use* weapons, they *are* the weapons. Examples include guns that can identify targets and shoot autonomously, flying drones that can deliver explosive charges to precise locations, and land mines that explode only when specific enemy vehicles are within range. The possibilities are so disturbing that significant efforts are under way by the United Nations and the military establishment to study the ethics and efficacy of using such precise munitions to support or replace personnel in war zones.[16] The current consensus is that as a matter of caution, a human should be "in the loop" for all targeting decisions before pulling the trigger, but it's not entirely clear that this is practical, or ethically defensible, since requiring such review may put lives at risk.

In contrast to some other, more clear-cut applications of AI, robotics shades from simple devices that perform rote actions (as are common in factories) to complex systems that sense their environment, reason, take action, and adjust their plans in response to new observations, so the boundaries of the field are far from clear. But it's helpful to bear in mind that actual progress lags behind public perception considerably. It's easy to shoot a video of an engaging robot with big eyes and an expressive face interacting in socially appropriate ways with a trained demonstrator, but for the most part these systems are far more fragile than people expect, at least so far. A more realistic and comical introduction to the state of the art is a video of robotic mishaps compiled and set to music by the *IEEE Spectrum* magazine, available on YouTube.[17]

What is computer vision?

As you might expect, computer vision is primarily focused on equipping computers with the ability to "see," in the sense of interpreting visual images. Work in the field of computer vision has paralleled the transition from symbolic systems to machine learning. Early efforts focused on crafting algorithms that used specialized knowledge of visual images and descriptions of objects of interest to look for semantically meaningful elements like lines, regions, and so on, which were often then aggregated into larger and more general entities. For instance, a program designed to identify a chair might look for legs, a seat, a back, and the like. But the more modern approach is to use machine learning, often specialized types of neural nets (called convolutional neural nets, or CNNs), to build models of objects from large collections of examples. Very loosely speaking, CNNs look for patterns in small, overlapping sections of an image, then can spread what they "learn" first to neighboring sections and then to progressively larger regions of the image.

Using these techniques, recent progress in the field has been quite rapid. For instance, accuracy on the annual ImageNet

Large Scale Visual Recognition Challenge, whose goal is to detect two hundred types of objects and localize them ("point them out") in 150,000 photographs containing a thousand object categories, has increased dramatically. Error rates are in the range of 5 percent, down from several times that only a few years ago.[18] The contest is now expanding to the identification of objects in videos and to more narrative descriptions of scenes, such as "The boy kicked the ball but missed the goal."

But the promise of this field extends beyond just visual imagery. A different way to think about computer vision, or visual processing in general, is that it takes as input flat, two-dimensional images representing light reflected off of three-dimensional surfaces, then interprets or reconstructs a model of the original scene. It may reconstruct a scene based on, for instance, multiple images from different viewpoints (stereo vision), knowledge of geometry and physics of light, reflectivity of various surfaces, and an understanding of the characteristics of real-world objects (people usually ride horses, not the other way around). The real, three-dimensional world obeys certain rules of composition, and these rules constrain the simplified two-dimensional view projected to the human eye or a digital camera. (These are the rules that optical illusions violate.) However, the same techniques have much broader application. While our eyes and most cameras sample reflected light, there are all sorts of sensors that collect data about the real world beyond what humans can see. Special devices, for instance, can measure infrared (heat), and reflected signals (e.g., radar and vibrations). The same basic rules and techniques that are used to process light, suitably adapted, can be applied to interpreting and reconstructing scenes based on these invisible signals.

There are "scenes" that obey certain physical constraints and commonalities, but can't in principle be seen at all (though using computer-based tools we can "visualize" them). Examples are the location and shape of oil formations underground, brain tumors, and imperfections in concrete dams under stress. As long as we have sufficient knowledge regarding the material characteristics of the domain we are examining, and have some method to collect signals that project these domains into images in ways that we understand, we can use computer vision techniques, broadly construed, to process them. In principle, neither the scenes nor the images need be physical. As long as the domains obey certain rules, and the images represent a lower-dimensional array of data points known to correspond to elements of the domain, the data can be processed to provide insight into the structure of the domain.[19]

In other words, computers can "see" things that we can't. This isn't as mystical as it sounds—the same is true of lots of animals. For instance, bats see using reflected sounds, and most birds are capable of seeing colors that humans can't, a skill they use to select mates, signal hunger, and foil nest parasites.[20]

What are the main applications of computer vision technology? A myriad of real-world problems depends on identifying and locating objects of interest in a given setting. Seemingly simple tasks, such as swinging a hammer at nails, stacking dishes, painting houses, mowing lawns, and picking ripe fruit depend on knowing where things are. The technology to act on this information—basic mechanical engineering and robotics—has been available for some time, but has been limited to environments where objects of interest were in predefined, fixed positions, such as on factory floors. But the recent advances in computer vision make it possible to perform physical tasks such as these in less structured, real-world environments. Over the next few decades, we are likely to witness a dramatic expansion of the classes of tasks—and therefore jobs—that can be performed by machines, as I will explore in later chapters.

A second major area of application is to information itself. We've largely completed a transition from physical, paper-based methods of capturing and communicating information (text, diagrams, pictures, and so on) to managing data in electronic form. But the data we are collecting, storing, and sharing is becoming increasingly visual in nature. The development of the digital camera, particularly when integrated into ubiquitous communications devices such as smartphones, has lowered the cost of taking and sharing photos to near zero, so instead of tapping out "I'm visiting the Golden Gate Bridge with my parents" on a tiny keyboard, many people simply click and send a picture. As a result, the proportion of visual information flowing through the Internet has ballooned. Video alone is projected to comprise 84 percent of all Internet traffic by 2018, according to a recent industry study.[21]

The problem is that unlike textual data, which we can interpret electronically for purposes of cataloging and retrieval, we have no way to manage pictures and videos unless they come labeled at the source or are categorized by a human. (You might be surprised to learn that when you do a Google search for images, you aren't actually searching the pictures themselves but rather the accompanying labels and text that suggest what may appear. This is why such searches are much less accurate than web page retrieval.) So as the bulk of electronic data shifts from textual to visual forms, we are in danger of "going dark" on the information flowing through our expanding digital networks.

But computer vision techniques offer the promise to manage all this automatically. Face recognition programs are already used for purposes as diverse as national security to flagging your friends in Facebook pictures. But soon the ability to interpret and label images will expand to include nearly every recognizable object, event, product, person, or scene that you may care to inquire about. Computer vision technology may arrive just in time to help us from drowning in an ocean of our own information.

What is speech recognition?

In contrast to humans, who presumably spoke before they wrote, computer use of language has been the other way around. Speech recognition is considerably more difficult than processing written language, in large part because of the variability and noise inherent in audio streams of spoken language. Separating the "signal" from the "noise," and transcribing it into the proper written words, is a daunting task for humans as well as computers, as any consumer of closed-captioning on TV can attest. But separating the vocalizations from background sounds is only the start of the problem. As early researchers in this field quickly discovered, there's no obvious break between words, contrary to what you may think when you listen to someone talk. Considerable meaning is also conveyed by how you vary your volume and tone (called "prosody" by linguists). In English, you can change the meaning of an utterance completely by raising your pitch at the end of a sentence—consider the difference between the way you say, "This is true" and "This is true?" Then there's the problem of distinguishing homonyms—different words or phrases that sound the same, such as "died" and "dyed." Who the speaker is, the domain of discourse, the previous context (if any), different voices, cadences, speed, and inflections further complicate this task.

The problem of recognizing speech differs fundamentally from interpreting a picture in that the former presents a single variable (sound waves) that changes dynamically over time, while the latter is a snapshot (so to speak) of reflected light in two dimensions at a single point in time. The information contained in the data is also fundamentally different. Speech is a man-made artifact intended to communicate a thought or idea as expressed in a specific sequence of words that are encoded as human-generated sounds. Sometimes this is enhanced with additional information—expressed through tonality, pacing, accent, vocabulary, and so on—that may signal the emotional state of speakers, their status relative to listeners, or their "tribal affiliation." (Except in rare circumstances, modern speech recognition systems ignore these secondary aspects of spoken language in favor of identifying the textual content.)

By contrast, pictures are naturally occurring patterns that obey the laws of physics. Thus different tools and techniques can be appropriately applied.

With all these challenges, it's a miracle that the problem can be solved at all. Most early speech recognition efforts attempted to simplify the task by limiting the vocabulary, operating in a simplified domain (like playing chess), requiring the speaker to pause between words, and either designing for a specific speaker or requiring extensive training sessions (for both the human speaker and the machine).[22]

In an attempt to jump-start progress in this field, in 1971 DARPA funded a five-year competition for continuous speech recognition (meaning no pauses between words) using a vocabulary of at least one thousand words. Whether any of the contestants succeeded was a matter of controversy, and the agency declined to renew funding following this initial term until it revived its interest nearly ten years later in 1984.[23] While the teams in this contest used a variety of different techniques, most could be roughly described as attempts to codify and bring to bear the accepted wisdom from a variety of fields, like syntax, phonetics, acoustics, and signal processing.

During the 1980s, a statistical technique called hidden Markov modeling (HMM) was applied to the speech recognition problem, with promising results. Informally, HMMs process the stream of sound dynamically (from left to right, so to speak), continually computing and updating the probability that one or more interpretations is the correct answer. This led to several commercially available speech recognition products, most prominently NaturallySpeaking from Dragon Systems (now part of Nuance Communications, Inc.).[24] While a significant improvement over previous efforts, this approach (at least in its earlier years) was still insufficiently accurate for widespread adoption of the technology.

More recently, the application of modern machine learning techniques—once again driven by the ability to capture and analyze large collections of speech samples—increased the precision and utility of these systems. In 2009, a group of researchers at the University of Toronto collaborated with IBM Research to apply machine learning techniques to the problem, reducing error rates by a remarkable 30 percent.[25] The improved results found a key use in smartphones as an alternative way to issue commands and enter data, thereby fueling an explosion of interest and research in the field.

Once again, the combination of more powerful computers, access to large amounts of training data, and machine learning techniques conspired to crack the problem and to deliver systems of practical and commercial importance. While the current state of the art in computer speech recognition is decidedly less capable than human speakers, the utility of this technology for limited domains is quite impressive, for example, in Google Voice and Apple's Siri, each available on the respective company's smartphones.

What is natural language processing?

A primary distinguishing factor between humans and other animals is our ability to use language. We use our words not only to communicate but also to help us think, remember, assign things to categories, and label individuals. Language serves not only to describe but also to educate, create, imagine, indicate intentions, make commitments, and identify people of similar heritage, among many other things. Like us, languages evolve and tailor themselves to our needs, almost as though they were living creatures in their own right.

There are so many competing theories about the evolution of language that the Linguistic Society of Paris actually banned discussion of the origins of language in 1866.[26] (Presumably, these Parisians loosened up at some point.) More recently, the legendary linguist Noam Chomsky (among others) questioned whether language evolved at all or was the result of a single, sudden individual mutation.[27] But one prominent theory is that language arose as a natural extension of gestures as a means of communication—ones performed with the tongue and mouth instead of the hands and arms. And indeed, gesturing and talking frequently co-occur in common use. (Some people have considerable trouble articulating their thoughts while sitting on their hands.) The appeal of this innovation as an aid to hunting and gathering is obvious: you free up your limbs to use for other purposes, and you can communicate without being in the line of sight. Better language means more food, so the motivation to bone up, so to speak, must have been strong. Not to mention the selective advantages language confers in promoting romance, trading, training, and codifying social conventions (rules and laws), which are reasons enough for it to catch on like wildfire, regardless of its origins.

But none of this has anything to do with machines or computers. While we talk about *computer languages,* the use of the term for these formal constructions is little more than an analogy, similar to the terms *machine learning* or *information superhighway.* Computer languages are designed for one purpose: to make it easier to program computers in a precise and unambiguous way. Programs that process computer languages, called compilers, are really formal methods for converting a more abstract but nonetheless rigorous specification of some computational process into a form that can be executed on a particular computing device.[28] You don't use Java (a popular computer language) to write poetry.

That said, there's a strong relationship between computer and human languages—or so people have believed until fairly recently. Descriptive linguists have long sought to codify the structure of language, dating back at least to the Indian grammarian Panini, who codified the syntax of the Sanskrit language into 3,996 rules in the fourth century BCE. And indeed, today we continue to teach grammar in, well, grammar school. But as every student quickly discovers, the rules don't always hold—you have to remember lots of exceptions. What these didactic failures indicate is that our attempts to reduce language to rules is at best an oversimplification, and at worst, just plain faulty.

But given the nearly universally accepted view that language obeys syntactic rules, it's no surprise that early researchers in computational linguistics approached the problem of processing natural (human) language on a computer by codifying it into a more sophisticated form of the same basic word categories and sentence structures you learned in school: nouns, verb phrases, subordinate clauses, and the like. (I was one of these people, having done my PhD thesis in this field in the late 1970s.) To be frank, this approach didn't work particularly well, mainly because it was insufficiently flexible to deal with just the sort of exceptions and common usages that plagued the rules you learned in school. Simply resolving references—deciding what a word or phrase, which may hold different meanings even within the same sentence, refers to—often involves knowledge and context far beyond the immediate text. (Linguists call this "anaphora.") I can direct you to sit in *this* chair instead of *that* chair, but without some knowledge of the physical context, there's no way to know which chairs I may be talking about. And while individual sentences and phrases may be susceptible to diagramming, dialog and conversation between multiple parties is another matter entirely. The plain truth is that there's clearly more (or less) going on than is captured by formal grammatical analysis.

And so, the processing of natural language by computer limped along for many decades until someone tried a completely different approach: machine learning, and more particularly statistical machine learning methods, as I described in chapter 2. While earlier approaches required the hand-crafting of rules, the new approach mainly required access to large bodies of text, and such "corpora," as collections of text are called, became larger and easier to gather as more and more written language was available in computer-readable form.

But all this analysis is useless until you try to do something with it—sentence diagrams, after all, are just line drawings with words attached until you employ them for some purpose, like moving subordinate clauses around. So work in the field focused on some problems of considerable practical significance, such as translating text from one language to another, generating summaries of documents, or answering questions, usually from a database of facts about some area of interest.

To focus on translation as an example, the big advantage is that you can start with pairs of correctly translated text to learn from, with limited need for other forms of knowledge or information about the subject matter. By automatically finding correlations between the source and target examples, statistical machine translation programs (as they are called) can learn not only the underlying structure of the input samples but how these correlate with the correct translation in the output samples.[29] These techniques don't definitively say that one phrase translates into another, but they provide a probability that various potential translations are correct.

Now it may seem counterintuitive that a computer program, with no real-world experience and no knowledge of what the text is about, could do a reasonable job of translating one language into another, much less beat out a computer program crafted by a human who is an expert speaker of both languages. But given enough examples, that's exactly what these systems can do. One of the remarkable achievements of modern AI could be couched as a discovery in search of an explanation: how simply finding correlations between enough examples can yield insights and solve problems at a super-human level, with no deeper understanding or causal knowledge about a domain. It raises the possibility that our human efforts at explanation are little more than convenient fictions, grand yet often imperfect summaries of myriad correlations and facts beyond the capacity of the human mind to comprehend. Yet, the success of machine translation, along with numerous other problem domains currently under study by

AI researchers using similar methods, suggests that the way we organize our thoughts may be only one of many possible ways to understand our world—and indeed may not be the best way. In general, what machine translation programs actually learn and how they perform their task is currently as incomprehensible and impenetrable as the inner workings of the human brain.

Notes

1. For a comprehensive review, see Bruno Siciliano and Oussama Khatib (eds.), *Springer Handbook of Robotics*, (New York: Springer Science+Business Media, 2008). As of this writing, an updated edition is scheduled for release 2017.
2. See NASA's Hubble space telescope service missions: http://www .nasa.gov/mission_pages/hubble/servicing/index.html.
3. John Kelley, "Study: Hubble Robotic Repair Mission Too Costly," Space.com, December 7, 2004, http://www.space.com/579-study-hubble-robotic-repair-mission-costly.html.
4. http://www.nasa.gov/mission_pages/mars/missions/index.html (last updated July 30, 2015).
5. DARPA Tactical Technology Office, DARPA Robotics Challenge (DRC), http://www.theroboticschallenge.org.
6. For instance, see Sam Byford, "This Cuddly Japanese Robot Bear Could Be the Future of Elderly Care," *Verge*, April 28, 2015, http://www.theverge.com/2015/4/28/8507049/robear-robot-bear-japan-elderly.
7. *Robot & Frank*, 2012, http://www.imdb.com/title/tt1990314/.
8. http://www.parorobots.com.
9. For instance, see Sherry Turkle, *Alone Together: Why We Expect More from Technology and Less from Each Other* (New York: Basic Books, 2012).
10. https://www.aldebaran.com/en/a-robots/who-is-pepper.
11. Furby: http://www.hasbro.com/en-us/brands/furby; AIBO: https:// en.wikipedia.org/wiki/AIBO.
12. http://www.irobot.com/For-the-Home/Vacuum-Cleaning/ Roomba.aspx.
13. See, for example, Pandey Nitesh Vinodbhai, "Manipulation of Sexual Behavior in Humans by Human Papilloma Virus," Indian Astrobiology Research Centre, http://vixra.org/pdf/1301.0194v1.pdf; and Sabra L. Klein, "Parasite Manipulation of the Proximate Mechanisms

That Mediate Social Behavior in Vertebrates," *Physiology & Behavior* 79, no. 3 (2003): 441–49, http://www.sciencedirect.com/science/article/pii/S003193840300163X.

14. https://en.wikipedia.org/wiki/Amazon_Robotics (last modified September 18, 2015).

15. http://www.robocup.org.

16. For more information, see the U.N. Lethal Autonomous Weapons Systems working group in Geneva, http://www.unog.ch/80256EE 600585943/(httpPages)/8FA3C2562A60FF81C1257CE600393DF6?O penDocument.

17. *A Compilation of Robots Falling Down at the DARPA Robotics Challenge, IEEE Spectrum* YouTube video, June 6, 2015, https://www.youtube .com/watch?v=g0TaYhjpOfo.

18. http://www.image-net.org.

19. The main constraint that the domains have to respect is to form what's called a "metric." Informally, a metric is a mathematical space that obeys the "triangle inequality": the shortest path between two points is a line that connects them; going through any point not on that line is a longer (less direct) path.

20. Cynthia Berger, "True Colors: How Birds See the World," *National Wildlife*, July 19, 2012, http://www.nwf.org/news-and-magazines/national-wildlife/birds/archives/2012/bird-vision.aspx.

21. Marina Lopes, "Videos May Make Up 84 Percent of Internet Traffic by 2018: Cisco," Reuters, June 10, 2014, http://www.reuters.com/article/us-internet-consumers-cisco-systems-idUSKBN0EL15E20140610.

22. For instance, see D. R. Reddy, L. D. Erman, R. O. Fennell, and R. B. Neely, "The Hearsay Speech Understanding System: An Example of the Recognition Process," in *Proceedings of the 3rd International Joint Conference on Artificial Intelligence* (Stanford, CA, 1973), 185–93 (San Francisco: Morgan Kaufmann Publishers Inc., 1973), http://ijcai.org/Past%20Proceedings/IJCAI-73/PDF/021.pdf.

23. National Research Council, "Developments in Artificial Intelligence," in *Funding a Revolution: Government Support for Computer Research*, (Washington, DC: National Academy Press, 1999), http://web.archive .org/web/20080112001018/http://www.nap.edu/readingroom/books/far/ch9.html#REF21.

24. http://www.nuance.com/index.htm.

25. John Markoff, "Scientists See Promise in Deep-Learning Programs," *New York Times*, November 23, 2012, http://www.nytimes. com/2012/11/24/science/scientists-see-advances-in-deep-learning-a-part-of-artificial-intelligence.html.

26. Thomas C. Scott-Phillips, "Evolutionary Psychology and the Origins of Language," *Journal of Evolutionary Psychology* 8(4) (2010):289–307, https://thomscottphillips.files.wordpress.com/2014/08/scott-phillips-2010-ep-and-language-origins.pdf.

27. Noam Chomsky, "Three Factors in Language Design," *Linguistic Inquiry* 36, no. 1 (2005): 1–22, http://www.biolinguistics.uqam.ca/Chomsky_05.pdf.

28. The actual process by which computer languages are executed is more nuanced than implied here. Some are "compiled"—translated into a so-called lower-level language in advance of being executed, while others are "interpreted" a little at a time as they are needed.

29. For links and an introduction to statistical machine translation, see http://www.statmt.org.

4

PHILOSOPHY OF ARTIFICIAL INTELLIGENCE

What is the philosophy of AI?

You might wonder why a field like AI seems to attract so much controversy. After all, other engineering disciplines—such as civil, mechanical, or electrical engineering—aren't typically the target of vociferous criticism from various branches of the humanities. Largely, these wounds are self-inflicted, as some practitioners, whether due to naiveté or in an effort to draw attention and funding, have made highly public overly broad claims for the generality of their results and optimistic forecasts of the future trajectory of the field.[1] That said, AI does pose real challenges to philosophical and religious doctrine about human uniqueness and our place in the universe. Intelligent machines offer the potential to shine an objective light on fundamental questions about the nature of our minds, the existence of free will, and whether nonbiological agents can be said to be alive. The prospect of actually settling many deep historical debates is both exciting and a little scary for those who ponder such issues. In the end, many of these issues come down to basic beliefs we have about ourselves, some of which resist scientific explanation (such as the existence of the human soul), or the Cartesian idea that mental events are somehow distinct from and independent of the physical world (dualism).

These intellectual questions are compounded by more pedestrian fears that AI may threaten the livelihoods if not the actual lives of many people. This concern, though legitimate, is fanned by the recurring theme in fiction and film of robot rebellion, dating back at least to the 1920 play by Czech playwright Karel Čapek, *R.U.R.*, also called *Rossum's Universal Robots*, which is credited with inventing the term *robot* (after the Czech word *robota*, meaning forced labor).[2]

In short, the philosophy of AI asks the question of whether computers, machines in general, or for that matter anything that is not of natural origin can be said to have a mind, and/or to think. The answer, simply put, depends on what you mean by "mind" and "think." The debate has raged on in various forms—unabated and unresolved—for decades, with no end in sight.

Here's some of the colorful history and arguments put forth by proponents and critics of the idea that machines can or do possess thinking minds.

What is "strong" versus "weak" AI?

I won't review the litany of claims made by AI researchers, but the most controversial of these can be summarized as a variant of what's called the "strong" versus the "weak" view on AI. In short, strong AI posits that machines do or ultimately will have minds, while weak AI asserts that they merely simulate, rather than duplicate, real intelligence. (The terms are sometimes misused, in my opinion, to describe the distinction between systems that exhibit general intelligent behavior versus those that are limited to a narrow domain, functioning as electronic idiot savants.) Stated another way, the distinction is between whether machines can be truly intelligent or simply able to act "as if" they are intelligent.

To demonstrate how confusing this matter can be, in this chapter I will attempt to convince you that you simultaneously hold contradictory views on this subject. If you do, it doesn't mean that you are crazy or muddled in your thinking; instead, I believe it indicates that we simply don't have an accepted intellectual framework sufficient to resolve this conflict—at least not yet. You and I may not, but I'm hopeful that at some point in the future, our children will.

Can a computer "think"?

The noted English mathematician Alan Turing considered this question in a 1950 essay entitled "Computing Machinery and Intelligence."[3] In it, he proposes, essentially, to put the issue to a vote. Constructing what he calls the "imitation game," he imagines an interrogator in a separate room, communicating with a man and a woman only through written communication (preferably typed), attempting to guess which interlocutor is the man and which is the woman. The man tries to fool the interrogator into thinking he is the woman, leaving the woman to proclaim her veracity (in vain, as Turing notes) in an attempt to help the interrogator make the correct identifications. Turing then invites the reader to imagine substituting a machine for the man, and a man for the woman. (The imitation game is now widely called the Turing Test.)[4]

Leaving aside the remarkable psychological irony of this famously homosexual scientist tasking the man with convincing the interrogator that he is a woman, not to mention his placing the man in the role of deceiver and the woman as truth teller, he goes on to ask whether it's plausible that the machine could ever win this game against a man. (That is, the machine is tasked with fooling the interrogator into thinking it is the man, while the man is telling the truth about who he is.) Contrary to the widely held belief that Turing was proposing an "entrance exam" to determine whether machines had come of age and become intelligent, he was actually speculating that our common use of the term *think* would eventually stretch sufficiently to be appropriately applied to certain machines or programs of adequate capability. His estimate of when this might occur was the end of the twentieth century, a remarkably accurate guess considering that we now routinely refer to computers as "thinking," mostly when we are waiting impatiently for them to respond. In his words, "The original question, 'Can machines think?' I believe to be too meaningless to deserve discussion. Nevertheless I believe that at the end of the century the use of words and general educated opinion will have altered so much that one will be able to speak of machines thinking without expecting to be contradicted."[5]

Is Turing right? Is this question too meaningless to deserve discussion? (And thus, by implication, this discussion is a waste of time?) Obviously, it depends on what we mean by "think."

We might consider thinking to be the ability to manipulate symbols to reason from initial assumptions to conclusions. From this perspective, it should be noncontroversial that computer programs, as we currently interpret them, are capable of such manipulations and therefore are capable of thinking. But surely just stirring up a brew of symbols isn't sufficient—it has to mean something or do something. Otherwise, there's not much justification for distinguishing one computer program from another, and any program that we interpret as processing symbols—no matter now trivial—would qualify as thinking, which doesn't seem right. But how does a computer program mean or do something?

The branch of philosophy and linguistics that deals with such questions, semiotics, studies the use of symbols for reasoning and communication. A distinction is commonly made between syntax, the rules for arranging and manipulating symbols, and semantics, the meaning of the symbols and rules. While syntax is pretty easy is to understand, semantics is not—even the experts don't agree on what "meaning" means. Most theories propose that meaning requires some way of relating the symbols themselves to the things they denote in the real world.

A quick example might help. You may think of numbers by themselves as having meaning, but they don't. To visualize why, consider the following symbols !, @, #, and $ as connected by an operator, +, that you can use to combine any pair of symbols from the set (=) into another symbol in the set:

$$! + ! = @$$
$$! + @ = \#$$
$$@ + ! = \#$$
$$! + \# = \$$$
$$\# + ! = \$$$
$$@ + @ = \$$$

Now you can play a little game of starting with a set of symbols and tracing it through the above rules to see where you wind up. Sounds like a good way to keep your five-year-old occupied for a few minutes, but it doesn't exactly command your attention as expressing a fundamental truth about the structure of our universe—until you substitute different symbols, leaving everything else the same:

$$1 + 1 = 2$$
$$1 + 2 = 3$$
$$2 + 1 = 3$$
$$1 + 3 = 4$$
$$3 + 1 = 4$$
$$2 + 2 = 4$$

Suddenly, everything makes sense. We all know what 1, 2, 3 and 4 mean, except for the minor inconvenience that they don't actually mean anything more or less than !, @, #, and $ do. They derive their meaning from how we connect them to other concepts or real-world objects. If we connect $ with any collection of four things, an expanded set of the above rules is exceedingly useful for solving certain problems of great practical significance. You can sit around manipulating symbols all day long and it doesn't mean a thing. In other words, loosely speaking, what you think doesn't matter, until you actually do something.

And to do something requires some connection between the actor manipulating the symbol system and something external to that actor. In the case of computer programs, this could (for instance) be figuring out how much you owe the phone company this month, the movement of a chess piece (physically or virtually), or a robot picking up a pencil. Only in this context can you say that the symbol manipulations have meaning.

Now, common arithmetic is one thing, but a vastly expanded concept of symbols and rules is a reasonable description of just about any computer program at some level, even if it's possible to make other interpretations of those same programs. It's an incredible eye-opener for most computer science majors when they first discover that all the math they ever learned in high school is simply a special case of some surprisingly easy to understand more general rules.[6]

So some critics of AI, most notably John Searle, professor of philosophy at the University of California at Berkeley, rightfully observe that computers, by themselves, can't "think" in this sense at all, since they don't actually mean or do anything—at best, they manipulate symbols. We're the ones associating their computations with the external world. But Searle goes further. He points out that even saying that computers are manipulating symbols is a stretch. Electrons may be floating around in circuits, but we are the ones interpreting this activity as symbol manipulation.

It's worth mentioning a more subtle argument put forth by some prominent thinkers, such as M. Ross Quillian.[7] While the symbols themselves may be devoid of any semantics, perhaps the meaning arises out of their relationships to other symbols, just as the definition of a word in a dictionary is expressed in terms of other words. While I regard this as an important insight and step forward, it seems insufficient. Aliens reading a dictionary could certainly glean a great deal about the nature of language, but it isn't going to give them a satisfactory understanding of what love is, for instance. Machine learning algorithms suffer from the same conceptual (though not practical) shortcoming—they reflect the complexity of the real world, but without some connection to that world, it's just so much unmoored structure.

Searle's arguments, and related ones by others, all make perfect intuitive sense until you apply them to people. We take it for granted that people think. But what's the difference between ideas swirling around in your brain and bytes zipping around in a computer? In both cases, information is going in, represented in some form that can plausibly be called symbolic (discrete nerve signals from your eyes, for example), getting processed, and coming back out (nerve signals to your hand to press keys on your keyboard, resulting in a spreadsheet of total monthly sales).

Searle argues that these must, in fact, be different things, but we just don't understand yet what the brain is doing. (He wisely abstains from speculating on what the actual difference is.)[8] It's important to understand what he's not saying. He isn't positing some magical property of the human mind that transcends science—his feet are firmly planted on the ground with a belief in the physical world as (mostly) deterministic, subject to measurement and rational explanation. He's just saying that something is happening in our brains that we don't understand yet, and that when we do (which he accepts as likely), it will pave the way for a satisfying explanation of what he believes are uniquely human phenomena—not just "thinking" but also consciousness, the feeling of experiencing things (what philosophers call "qualia"), sentience, and so on. He also isn't arguing that a computer program can never perform any particular task—be that to paint beautiful paintings, discover laws of nature, or console you on the loss of a loved one. But he believes that the program is *simulating* thinking, not *duplicating* the process that occurs in human minds when they engage in these activities. To Searle, a player piano isn't doing the same thing as a master musician when performing a Rachmaninoff concerto, even if it sounds the same. In short, Searle is saying that when it comes to computers, at least as they exist today, no one is home.

Despite the ongoing efforts of generations of AI researchers to explain away Searle's observations, in my opinion his basic point is right.[9] Computer programs, taken by themselves, don't really square with our commonsense intuition about what it means to think. They are "simply" carrying out logical, deterministic sequences of actions, no matter how complex, changing their internal configurations from one state to another. But here's where we get into trouble: if you believe that our brains are little more than symbol manipulators composed of biological material, then you are naturally forced to conclude that your brain, by itself, can't think either. Disconnect it from the outside world, and it would be doing just what a computer does. But that doesn't square with our commonsense intuition that even if we sit in a dark, quiet room, deprived of all input and output, we can still sit there and think. We can't have it both ways: if symbol manipulation is the basis of intelligence, either both people and machines can think (in principle, if not in practice today), or neither can.

But if you prefer to maintain the comforting conceit that we are special—different from machines in some fundamental way yet to be determined (as Searle believes), or that we are imbued with some mystical qualities quite distinct from the rest of the natural world, then you can cling to the notion that thinking is uniquely human, and machines are simply pretenders to our cognitive abilities. It's your choice. But before you make up your mind, bear in mind that there's an accumulating body of evidence chipping away at our seemingly obvious intuitions about our most quintessentially human abilities—for example, that we actually have free will.

Can a computer have free will?

Virtually everyone believes that humans, and possibly some animals, have free will, but can a machine or a computer also have free will? To answer this question, it's necessary to have some notion of what we mean by free will. There is a long intellectual and religious history of debate about the nature and existence of free will. (Wikipedia has an excellent article reviewing the various schools of thought and major arguments.)[10] Usually what we mean is that we have the ability to make considered choices, possibly swayed but not determined by forces outside of ourselves. So the first thing to observe is that we make a distinction between inside and outside: to understand free will, we have to wrap a box around what is "us" to separate it from what is "not us." But that alone is not enough. Inside the box, we must be free to consider our options without undue influence so we can make a thoughtful choice, without having a particular conclusion preordained or forced upon us. An important consequence of this concept is that our decisions must not, in principle, be predictable. If they were, we wouldn't really be making a free choice.

Now, you might assume that computers cannot have free will because they are different from us in two key respects. First, they work according to well-understood engineering principles and so can always be predicted. Second, they can't really be said to consider choices in the same sense that people do. The problem is, both of these assertions are questionable at best.

Let's start by digging into the concept of predictability. For the purposes of this discussion I'm going to assume, as most people do (at least in contemporary Western cultures), that the physical world operates in accordance with certain laws of nature, whether or not we know or can know what those laws are. This is not to say that everything is predetermined—indeed, randomness may in fact be a fundamental part of nature. But randomness is just that—random, not a free pass for things to happen in accordance with some grander plan or principle that is somehow outside of the laws of nature. Otherwise those plans would simply be part of the laws. In other words, there is no such thing as magic. Further, I'm going to assume that your mind arises from your brain, and your brain is a physical object subject to the laws of nature.

What exactly your mind is, or how it arises from the brain, doesn't matter for this discussion, as long as you accept that it does. Another way to say this is that given a particular state of mind, there will be an equally distinct state of the brain—two different incompatible thoughts or beliefs can't arise from a single physical arrangement of matter and energy in your brain. I'm not aware of any objective evidence to the contrary, but that doesn't mean for certain that these assumptions are correct—indeed, much of the historical debate over free will focuses on precisely these assumptions, so to some degree I've baked in my conclusions by taking these positions.

Now imagine that we put you in a room, police interrogation style, with a one-way mirror on the wall so a group of very smart future scientists can observe everything about you—including the state and behavior of every neuron in your brain. We then ask you to say out loud either "red" or "blue." But before you do, we challenge the scientists to predict which you are going to pick. Running their tests, simulation models, and whatever else they want, they demonstrate that they can correctly predict what you are going to say 100 percent of the time. From this, they proudly announce that you do not have free will—after all, no matter how hard you try, you can't fool them.

But you beg to differ, and demand an opportunity to demonstrate that, in fact, you are not so dull and predictable. First, you try to decide what you're going to pick, then explicitly change your mind. This doesn't work, because, of course, the scientists are able to predict that you are going to do this. But then you get an idea. You discover that if you sit very quietly, you can hear the scientists discussing their predictions. So the next time they ask you to pick a color, you listen in on their deliberations and learn what they have predicted. Then you simply pick the other color. Stymied by your inventiveness, they incorporate this into their models—that not only do you get to pick, but also that you have access to their prediction before you do so. There's nothing uncertain or unclear about this new wrinkle, but to their surprise, their enhanced model doesn't work. No matter how they try, you can still prove them wrong by picking the other color.

So how did you show them up? By expanding the "box" between the inside and outside of your thoughts—in this case, to include them. In short, if the box is big enough, what's inside it cannot in all circumstances predict what it will do, even though something completely outside the box can (in principle, as far as we know). As long as you can enlarge the box to include the prediction, no such prediction can always be correct.

Now, there's nothing in this argument that can't apply as well to a machine as to you. We can build a robot that does exactly what you did. No matter how we program that robot to make decisions, no matter how predictable that robot is, as long as it has access to an outside forecast of its own actions, that forecast can't always be correct. The robot can simply wait for that forecast, then do the opposite. So a sufficiently capable robot can't always be predicted, where "sufficiently capable" means it has access to the attempt to predict what it will do.

This is an example of what computer scientists call an undecidable problem—there is no effective algorithm that can solve the problem completely (meaning that it gives a correct answer in all cases). Note that this is an entirely different concept from the more widely known and similarly named uncertainty principle in physics, which states that your knowledge of both the position and momentum of a particle is limited in precision and inversely related. Undecidable problems really do exist. Probably the most famous one was formulated by none other than Alan Turing, and it is called the "halting problem." The halting problem is easy to state: can you write a program A that will examine any other program B along with its input and tell you whether or not B will eventually stop running? In other words, can A tell if B will ever finish and produce an answer? Turing showed that no such program A can exist, using an argument similar to the one above.[11]

So in practice, what actually happens? The program doesn't make a mistake—that is, give you a wrong answer. Instead, it simply never stops running. In the case of our future scientists, no matter how clever their prediction process, in some cases it will simply never reach a conclusion as to whether you are going to pick red or blue. This doesn't mean you don't get to pick your answer, just that they can't always tell in advance what you are going to pick. The scientists might cry foul, noting that they are never wrong, which is true. But you counter that never being wrong is not the same thing as being able to reliably predict your behavior.

So, it's not the case that a deterministic machine, whose behavior is completely specified and understood, can always be predicted. Any given state of a computer program may transition to its next state in an entirely predictable way, but surprisingly, we can't simply string knowledge of these states together to get a complete picture of what the program will ultimately do. And the same, of course, is true for you— in particular, you can never accurately predict your own behavior. It's possible that this is why we have the strong intuition that we have free will, but this is simply an interesting hypothesis, not a proven fact. Other possibilities are that our subjective sense of free will has arisen to serve some yet to be identified evolutionary purpose(s), like desiring sweets or being attracted to the opposite sex.

Now let's turn to the question of what it means for you to make a decision of your own volition. Just because you can make a choice doesn't mean you have free will. For instance, you could flip a coin to decide.

One of the clearest and most concise critiques of relying on chance to provide the wiggle room needed to explain free will is by contemporary thinker Sam Harris.[12] He argues that the whole idea that you can make a meaningful deliberate choice independent of outside or prior influences simply doesn't make any sense. He asks you to imagine two worlds. Both are exactly the same right up until you make a decision of your own free will, then they diverge by virtue of your choice. In one, you choose red and in the other you choose blue. Now, in what sense did you intentionally pick one rather than the other? Your thinking was exactly the same up until that precise moment, yet somehow you made a different choice. But, you might counter, you made up your own mind. Harris would reply, based on what? Something led up to your decision, presumably internal mental deliberations—otherwise your decision was simply determined by some process that, though possibly random, does not reflect anything resembling what we mean by deliberative intent. But that means that the "red" and "blue" worlds had already diverged before you decided. So let's move the starting line back to when you began to think about the problem—maybe that's when you exercised free will. But at that point you hadn't decided anything at all—in fact, you hadn't even begun to think about it. Harris concludes, reasonably enough, that free will in the sense of intentional choice, unfettered and undetermined by previous events, is nothing more than an illusion.

Now let's look at the question of how computers make decisions. Unlike people, we have a really good idea of how they work. Nonetheless, they can make choices without relying on randomness. They can weigh evidence, apply knowledge and expertise, make decisions in the face of uncertainty, take risks, modify their plans based on new information, observe the results of their own actions, reason (in the case of symbolic processing), or use what could reasonably be called intuition (for instance, by employing machine learning to inform their actions in the absence of any deeper understanding of causal relationships). And as IBM's Watson illustrates, they are capable of using metaphor and analogy to solve problems. Now, all of my descriptions superimpose somewhat anthropomorphic interpretations on what they are doing, but that's no less reasonable than describing your deliberations even though your thoughts are ultimately represented by some particular states of your brain.

Up until fairly recently, the idea that we could have access to our own internal reflections was simply a pipe dream, so philosophers could plausibly presume that there might be something magical, mysterious, or nonphysical about our mental processes. But experimental psychologists have unearthed new and disquieting evidence that our brains make decisions before our minds are consciously aware of them, just as they regulate our blood pressure without our conscious intervention. For instance, in 2008 a group of researchers asked test subjects to freely choose whether to push a button with their left or right hands. Using an fMRI brain scanner, they were able to predict which hand the subjects would use up to ten seconds before the subjects consciously made the decision.[13] So what does this say about the box we need to draw around "us" versus the external world? As we learn more and more about how our brains—as opposed to our minds—actually work, our private, mental world would seem to be shrinking into invisibility.

So if there's no such thing as free will, why should you ever try to do anything, for instance, to lose weight? Sam Harris goes on to make the interesting observation that you may not have any meaningful choice as to whether to diet or not, but one thing for sure is that if you don't try, you won't succeed. So even if free will does not exist, it doesn't get you off the hook for trying—that just goes hand in hand with actually doing.

To summarize, it's not clear whether, or what, it means for you to have free will—lots of smart people find it plausible that your sense of choice is nothing more than an illusion. Presumably your brain, as a physical object, plays by the same rules as the rest of the physical world, and so may be subject to inspection and analysis. And if your mind arises from your brain, at some level it too must operate according to some laws of nature, whether we understand those laws yet or not. Introducing randomness into the picture doesn't get around this problem, and neither does the peculiar fact that lots of deterministic processes are nonetheless not subject to prediction, even in principle. Finally, there's no reason other than wishful thinking to suggest that machines are in this regard any different from us. This is not to say that people and machines are equivalent in all respects—they clearly aren't. But when it comes to making choices, so far, at least, there aren't good reasons to believe they operate according to different natural or scientific principles.

So we're left with the following conclusion: either both people and computers can have free will, or neither can—at least until we discover some evidence to the contrary. Take your pick.

Can a computer be conscious?

As with free will, satisfying definitions of consciousness are notoriously elusive. The more we seem to learn about brain science, the more problematic the abstract notion of consciousness becomes. Some researchers tie consciousness to the role of emotional states and physical embodiment. Others have developed evidence that blocking communications across various parts of the brain will cause consciousness to cease. Studies of patients in vegetative states suggest that consciousness is not entirely black or white but can be somewhere in between, resulting in limited awareness and ability to respond to external events. Antonio Damasio, a cognitive neuroscientist at the University of Southern California, has developed an influential theory called the "somatic marker hypothesis," which in part proposes that broad linkages across our brains and bodies are the basis of sentience.[14] Giulio Tononi, who holds the Distinguished Chair in Consciousness Science at the University of Wisconsin–Madison, believes that consciousness arises from the wide integration of information within the brain.[15]

Until we have an objective way to define and test for human consciousness other than by simply observing others, there's no rational basis for believing that people are conscious but machines cannot be. But it's equally unjustified to assert that machines can be conscious. At the present time there's no credible way to establish whether computers and animals—or other people, for that matter—experience consciousness the same way we feel that we do.

This is a serious problem. Most of us would agree that hurting or killing a conscious being against its will is morally wrong. But what if it isn't conscious? I can build a machine that objects strongly to being turned off, but does that make doing so wrong? (I will discuss this issue further in the next section.)

That said, my personal opinion is that the notion of consciousness, or subjective experience more generally, simply doesn't apply to machines. I've certainly seen no evidence of it to date. And without some definitional guideposts to point to how we might even address the question, I'm lost. It's likely that machines will, at the very least, *behave* as if they are conscious, leaving us with some difficult choices about the consequences. And our children, who likely will grow up being tenderly cared for by patient, selfless, insightful machines, may very well answer this question differently than we might today.

Can a computer "feel"?

You might have noticed a common thread so far: that the answers to our questions hinged largely on whether you regard words like *intelligence, thinking,* and *feeling* as connoting something sacrosanct about humans (or at least biological creatures), or whether you are comfortable expanding their applicability to certain artifacts.

In this regard, our own language is working against us. The challenge posed by AI is how to describe, and therefore how to understand and reason about, a phenomenon never before encountered in human experience—computational devices capable of perception, reasoning, and complex actions. But the words that seem to most closely fit these new developments are colored with implications about humanity's uniqueness. To put this in perspective, it's been a few hundred years or so since we last faced a serious challenge to our beliefs about our place in the universe—the theory that we descended from less capable creatures. In some quarters, this proposal did not go down well. Yet today there is widespread (though not universal) acceptance of and comfort with the idea that we originated not through some sudden divine act of intentional creation but through the process of natural selection as noted by Darwin, among others.

Okay, we're animals—so what? It turns out that this seemingly simple shift in categories is a much bigger deal than you might expect. It ignited a raging debate that is far from settled, and AI is poised to open a new frontier in that war of words. At issue is what moral obligations, if any, do we have toward other living creatures? All of a sudden, they became distant relatives, not just resources put on earth for our convenience and use. Fundamental to that question is whether other animals feel pain, and whether we have the right to inflict it on them.

The logical starting point for determining if animals feel pain is to consider how similar or different they are from us. There is an extensive scientific literature studying the physiological manifestations of pain in animals, mainly focusing on how much their reactions mirror our own.[16] As you might expect, the more closely related those animals are to humans, the more congruent their reactions. But despite this growing body of knowledge, the plain fact is that no one knows for sure. Advocates for animal rights, such as Peter Singer, point out that you can't even know for sure whether other people feel pain, though most of us, with the possible exception of psychopaths and solipsists, accept this as true. In his words: "We ... know that the nervous systems of other animals were not artificially constructed—as a robot might be artificially constructed—to mimic the pain behavior of humans. The nervous systems of animals evolved as our own did, and in fact the evolutionary history of human beings and other animals, especially mammals, did not diverge until the central features of our nervous systems were already in existence."[17]

Many animal rights advocates take a better-safe-than-sorry approach to this question. What are the consequences of treating animals *as if* they feel pain versus the consequences of assuming they do not? In the former case, we merely impose some potentially unnecessary inconveniences and costs on ourselves, whereas in the latter case, we risk causing extreme and enduring suffering. But the underlying assumption in this debate is that the more similar animals are to us, the greater our moral obligation to act in what we perceive to be their independent interests.

Now let's apply this logic to machines. It's relatively simple to build a robot that flinches, cries out, and/or simply says, "Ouch, that hurts" when you pinch it. But as Peter Singer points out, does that say anything about whether it feels pain? Because we are able to look beyond its reactions to its internal structure, the answer is no. It reacts that way because that's what we designed it to do, not because it feels pain. (In chapter 8 I will consider the benefits and dangers of anthropomorphizing our creations.) While some people form inappropriate attachments to their possessions, such as falling in love with their cars, most of us recognize this as a misplaced application of our nurturing instinct. The tools we build are, well, tools—to be used for our betterment as we see fit. Whether those tools are simple and inanimate, like a hammer, or more complex and active, like an air-conditioner, does not seem to bear on the question. These gadgets lack the requisite breath of life to deserve moral consideration. And there's little reason to see computers as any different in this regard. Since computers are so different from us (at least today) and are designed by us for specific purposes (as opposed to naturally occurring), it seems logical to say they don't, and most likely never will, have real feelings.

Now let me convince you of the exact opposite. Imagine that you (or your spouse) give birth to a beautiful baby girl—your only child. Unfortunately, shortly after her fifth birthday, she develops a rare degenerative neurological condition that causes her brain cells to die prematurely, one by one. Luckily for her (and you), by that time the state of the art in neurological prosthetics has advanced considerably, and she is offered a novel treatment. Once every few months, you can take her to the doctor for a scan and neuronal replacement of any brain cells that have ceased to fully function in the interim. These remarkable implants, an amalgam of microscopic circuits and wires powered by body heat, precisely mirror the active properties of natural neurons. In an ingenious technique that mimics the human immune system, they are inserted intravenously, then they home in on neurons in the final stages of death, dissolving and replacing then in situ. The results are spectacular—your little girl continues to grow and thrive, experiencing all the trials and triumphs associated with a normal childhood.

After many years of regular outpatient visits no more noteworthy than regular dental checkups, the doctor informs you that there is no longer any need to continue. You ask if this means she's cured, but the answer isn't quite what you expected—the doctor nonchalantly informs you that 100 percent of her neurons have been replaced. She's a fully functioning, vivacious, and passionate teenager—apparently with an artificial brain.

Her life proceeds normally until one day, as a young adult, she enters one of her musical compositions into a prestigious competition for emerging composers. Upon learning of her childhood disability, the other contestants petition the panel of judges to disqualify her on the basis that her piece violates one of the contest rules—that all entries be composed without the assistance of computers or other artificial aids. After an all-too-brief hearing, she is referred to a parallel contest track for computer music. It pains you deeply to see your daughter so devastated. How, she cries, is she any different from the player in the violin competition who has an artificial elbow due to a skiing accident, or the one whose corneal implants permit her to sight-read without glasses?

Whether or not you concur with the judges' decision, a sober consideration of the facts unbiased by your feeling of kinship forces you to admit that they at least have a point—your daughter's brain is a man-made computing device, even if it produces normal human behavior and development in every relevant respect. Nonetheless, you would be loath to conclude that she is nothing more than a clever artifact, incapable of real feelings, undeserving of moral considerations or human rights.

So where does this leave us? On the one hand, our intuitions lead us to believe that machines, no matter how sophisticated, raise no ethical concerns in their own right. On the other, we can't comfortably exclude certain entities from the community of living things based solely on what materials they are composed of. My personal opinion, not universally shared, is that what's at issue here is little more than a decision we get to make as to whom, or to what, we choose to extend the courtesy of our empathy. Our conviction that other people or animals feel, or the fact that we love our relatives more strongly than strangers, is simply nature's way of guiding our behavior toward its own peculiar ends, an argument won not through logic and persuasion but through instinct and impulse. Though today we might be justifiably proud of our computational creations, it's hard to imagine why we should care about their welfare and achievements other than for how they benefit us. But nature has a sneaky habit of getting its way. Can machines feel? Who cares? The important question is whether highly sophisticated self-reproducing adaptive devices, which we may be in the process of creating, might inherit the earth—regardless of our role in helping this happen. Like so many species before us, we may simply be a stepping-stone to something we can't comprehend.

Notes

1. Stuart Armstrong, Kaj Sotala, and Sean S. OhEigeartaigh, "The Errors, Insights and Lessons of Famous AI Predictions—and What They Mean for the Future," Future of Humanity Institute, University of Oxford, 2014, http://www.fhi.ox.ac.uk/wp-content/uploads/FAIC.pdf.

2. Karel Čapek and Claudia Novack-Jones, *R.U.R. (Rossum's Universal Robots)* (New York: Penguin Classics, 2004).

3. Turing, A.M. (1950). "Computing machinery and intelligence," Mind, 59, 433-460, http://www.loebner.net/Prizef/TuringArticle.html.

4. If you've heard a more politically correct sanitized version of the Turing Test, namely, that it's about a machine attempting to convince a human that it is human, I encourage you to read Turing's original paper.

5. Section 6 of Turing's paper.

6. In mathematics, the study of systems of symbols and rules like these is called "abstract algebra."

7. R. Quillian, "Semantic Memory" (PhD diss., Carnegie Institute of Technology, 1966), reprinted in Marvin Minsky, *Semantic Information Processing* (Cambridge, MA: MIT Press, 2003).

8. For a short, informal expression of Searle's views, see Zan Boag, "Searle: It Upsets Me When I Read the Nonsense Written by My Contemporaries," *NewPhilosopher*, January 25, 2014, http://www.newphilosopher.com/articles/john-searle-it-upsets-me-when-i-read-the-nonsense-written-by-my-contemporaries/.

9. John Preston and Mark Bishop, eds., *Views into the Chinese Room: New Essays on Searle and Artificial Intelligence* (Oxford: Oxford University Press, 2002).

10. http://en.wikipedia.org/wiki/Free_will.

11. The gist of Turing's argument is that there are as many different computer programs as integers, but those programs taken together behave in as many different ways as there are rational numbers—and you can't count rationals with integers. Alan Turing, "On Computable Numbers, with an Application to the Entscheidungsproblem," *Proceedings of the London Mathemathical Society*, Vol. s2–42, Issue 1, (1937): 230–65.

12. Sam Harris, *Free Will* (New York: Free Press, 2012).

13. Chun Siong Soon, Marcel Brass, Hans-Jochen Heinze, and John-Dylan Haynes, "Unconscious Determinants of Free Decisions in the

Human Brain," *Nature Neuroscience* 11 (2008): 543–45, http://www.nature.com/neuro/journal/v11/n5/abs/nn.2112.html.

14. For instance, see Antonio Damasio, *The Feeling of What Happens: Body and Emotion in the Making of Consciousness* (Boston: Harcourt, 1999).

15. Giulio Tononi, *Phi: A Voyage from the Brain to the Soul* (New York: Pantheon, 2012).

16. For an excellent and very concise review of this issue, see Lynne U. Sneddon, "Can Animals Feel Pain?" http://www.wellcome.ac.uk/en/pain/microsite/culture2.html.

17. Peter Singer, *Animal Liberation*, 2nd ed. (New York: Avon Books, 1990), page 10, http://www.animal-rights-library.com/texts-m/singer03.htm.

5

ARTIFICIAL INTELLIGENCE AND THE LAW

How will AI affect the law?

AI will significantly impact a wide variety of human activities and have a dramatic influence on many fields, professions, and markets. Any attempt to catalog these would necessarily be incomplete and go quickly out of date, so I will focus on just one as an illustration: the potential effects of AI on the nature, practice, and application of the law. In this review, I will cover how AI will change the practice of law as well as the way laws will be formulated and administered, and why the emergence of AI systems will require modification and extension of current legal concepts and principles. But bear in mind that a similar analysis can be done for a broad array of fields and activities, from prospecting to plate tectonics, accounting to mathematics, traffic management to celestial dynamics, press releases to poetry.

How will AI change the practice of law?

To understand how AI is likely to impact the practice of law, it's helpful to understand how it is currently practiced, at least in the United States. The American Bar Association (ABA), an influential trade organization, was formed in 1878 by seventy-five prominent lawyers from around the country, and today has over four hundred thousand members.[1] As of 2014, there were nearly 1.3 million lawyers licensed to practice in the United States, 75 percent of whom were in private practice.[2] While the ABA engages in many laudable efforts to ensure that the practice of law meets high ethical and professional standards, its primary mission is to promote the interests of lawyers ("Goal 1: Serve Our Members").[3] Like virtually all professional guilds, the ABA, along with a patchwork of state and local counterparts, influences if not controls who can practice law, how they can promote their services, and how much they can charge. It serves as the gatekeeper to the profession by accrediting law schools, from which most states require aspiring lawyers to obtain a law degree before they take their bar exams and therefore become licensed to practice law. To maintain this control, the ABA proposes model rules regarding the unauthorized practice of law, which is considered a criminal—as opposed to civil—offense in most jurisdictions. Judge Richard Posner (U.S. Court of Appeals, Seventh Circuit) has described the legal profession as "a cartel of providers of services relating to society's laws."[4]

In essence, society has struck a bargain with the legal profession: it is permitted to operate a monopoly, controlling access and maintaining price integrity, in return for making legal assistance available to those unable to afford a lawyer "pro bono" (free), mainly via a network of public and private legal aid services. The problem is, the profession has largely failed to keep up its end of the bargain. As of 2009, a study found that one legal aid attorney was available to serve 6,415 low-income people, while attorneys in private practice available for those above the poverty level served only 429 people.[5] Other studies show that 30 percent of low-income Americans have little or no access to legal assistance, and even nonindigent citizens cannot afford to pursue appropriate legal redress a significant percentage of the time.[6] Not to mention that in my experience, it's just plain expensive to hire a lawyer, and often difficult to manage him or her when you do.

Technology to serve the legal profession has advanced tremendously over the past few decades, if not centuries. The ability to collect and widely disseminate legal statutes and judicial decisions that serve as precedents is a relatively recent occurrence. As professor Oliver Goodenough of Vermont Law School has observed, Abraham Lincoln's practice of law was largely limited by the number of books he could carry on his horse, and court arguments in his time were often little more than reciting aphorisms like "What's good for the goose is good for the gander."[7] Today, not only do attorneys have near-instant access to virtually all case law, a wide variety of information systems support their work in drafting contracts, briefs, and all manner of legal documents.

Yet, those working to provide tools that streamline and reduce costs for legal professionals run into a simple problem: people paid by the hour don't like things that save them time. Lawyers are disinclined to adopt technology that speeds their work unless they are paid on contingency or through fixed fees. In other words, the main impediment to making legal services more broadly available and affordable is the economic structure of the legal profession. Because of this, many lawyers are understandably resistant to any technology, no matter how effective and efficient, that can help people to help themselves. But creating that technology is exactly where AI is heading.

While television mainly portrays lawyers earnestly representing their clients in front of judges and juries, in the real world few see the inside of a courtroom on a regular basis. The plain fact is that most legal activities are straightforward transactions, not disputes—such as drafting contracts, filing for divorce, purchasing a house (which requires a lawyer in many locales), applying for a patent, petitioning for a change of immigrant status, forming a corporation, declaring bankruptcy, writing a will or estate plan, or registering a trademark. And a very large proportion of the common services that lawyers perform are sufficiently routine that a fairly straightforward AI system can do them as well as or better than the average lawyer.[8] At the very least, such automated systems can handle the bulk of the work, reserving only the exceptions and complex cases for human review. The impact of automation—whether AI-based or not—is at least one underlying reason that enrollment in law schools, and the starting salaries of lawyers, has been dropping, precipitating a crisis in the profession.[9] Lawyers are experiencing the same "do it yourself" pressures that are gutting other industries whose business model has historically been driven largely by restricted access to information and relatively repetitive skills, such as booking travel. (Employment of travel agents is projected to drop an additional 12 percent over the next decade, compared to an expected 11 percent growth in overall employment.)[10]

Historically, the most obvious way to assist consumers with legal matters was to provide them with sample "fill in the blanks" forms. As a general matter, these are considered legal, though even that has been challenged by at least one bar association.[11] It was a short hop from providing such forms on paper to providing them online over the Internet. But from there, the trouble starts. If you are going to provide the forms, why not help the customer fill them out? And since lots of "blanks" are contingent, based on the contents of other "blanks," why not have the software skip the inappropriate ones? (For example, if you don't have children, you don't need to fill in information about child support on a divorce form.) But even this obvious step toward efficiency, using so-called decision trees, has been ferociously resisted by the legal profession. While it's generally acceptable for software programs to provide forms, it is not acceptable for them to do "document preparation." LegalZoom, a leading company that provides document preparation to consumers over the Internet, has been the target of numerous lawsuits alleging that it is engaged in the unauthorized practice of law.[12] Other valuable online legal services hide under the fig leaf that they are "referral services," which are permitted, though heavily regulated.[13] One such example is FairDocument, which focuses on estate planning.

FairDocument pitches itself as a lawyer referral service: first, its sophisticated algorithms interview you about your desires and needs, then the company provides a draft document to an independent lawyer, who reviews and completes the work (often with few or no changes). Then you pay the lawyer a fee—usually far less than typical estate attorneys charge—and FairDocument gets a cut.[14]

Given these headwinds, many technologists focus their automation efforts on peripheral problems, such as resolving disputes before they rise to the level of a legal action or get to trial. Courts and litigants have long encouraged the use of quasi-judicial pretrial resolution forums to reduce caseloads (known as alternative dispute resolution). If conflicts can be resolved privately, all parties are better off. To date, this involves the use of professional negotiators, mediators, and arbitrators essentially acting as private judges. However, new techniques are moving the role of technology beyond simply facilitating communication between the parties to actively participating in the resolution process.[15] Such systems employ game theory, analysis of successful outcomes, and negotiation strategies to resolve issues using methodology that litigants perceive to be objective and unbiased, making them more amenable to settlement.

While most of the systems demonstrated to date are research prototypes, some new companies, such as Cognicor and Modria, are applying these techniques to lower-stakes disputes like customer complaints and disagreements between buyers and sellers in online marketplaces.[16] Modria claims to resolve up to 90 percent of claims for its customers without the need to escalate the issue to a human customer service representative. Its software collects and analyzes the relevant information related to the dispute, even incorporating such subjective considerations as the complainant's purchasing history and prior business relationships with the parties involved, then uses a set of guidelines, including policies for refunds, returns, exchanges and charge-backs, to propose and potentially implement a mutually acceptable resolution.

How is AI used to help lawyers?

But the situation is completely different when the economics favor adoption of technology by lawyers. One such thriving area is called "e-discovery." In the course of litigation, both plaintiffs and defendants are permitted access to each other's relevant documents to look for evidence pertinent to the case. The problem is, this document production may be voluminous. Until fairly recently, the review of discovery documents was done by lawyers, or at least trained specialists such as paralegals. Many fresh law school graduates have been horrified to find themselves assigned the task of reading endless stacks of documents, a rite of passage viewed with dread, analogous to a medical student's grueling hospital internship. Due to the ease of maintaining electronic documents (indeed, it's a challenge to get rid of them), not to mention that so much of today's business is transacted in electronic form, the volumes produced in response to discovery requests can be staggering. For example, in one antitrust case, Microsoft produced over 25 million pages of documents, all of which had to be reviewed not only for relevance but often to redact nonmaterial confidential information which might be subject to a so-called protective order prohibiting even the client from viewing the contents.[17] How could this possibly be completed in a practical time frame at a reasonable cost (meaning one that the lawyer's clients can stomach)? AI to the rescue.

A technique called "predictive coding" can permit a computer to perform this mind-numbing task with speed, diligence, and accuracy far exceeding that of human reviewers. First, human attorneys review a set of sample documents statistically selected to represent the characteristics of the entire collection. Then a machine learning program goes to work identifying criteria that will permit it to match the human performance as closely as possible. The criteria may involve everything from simple phrase matching to very sophisticated semantic analysis of the text, context, and participants. The newly trained program is then run on a subset of the remaining items to produce a new set of documents, and these in turn are reviewed by the attorneys. This process iterates until the program is capable of selecting adequately relevant documents on its own. (The technique is similar to the way email spam filters are tuned using feedback from users who mark messages as "junk.") E-discovery has spawned an entire mini-industry of service providers. Indeed, Microsoft itself recently acquired Equivio, one of the leading companies in the field.[18]

This is but one example of AI applications that support lawyers, though it is arguably the most commercially developed. Other efforts include ways of predicting the outcome of lawsuits. For instance, a recent effort to apply machine learning techniques to predicting the outcome of U.S. Supreme Court decisions was able to correctly guess the judges' decisions more than 70 percent of the time, using data only from cases prior to the case predicted. It does so by analyzing the voting behavior of each individual justice from a database of sixty-eight thousand such votes.[19] Such information is critical for lawyers in preparing their cases and advising their clients.

What is computational law?

So far I have covered the effects of AI on lawyers and the practice of law, but perhaps its most meaningful impact will ultimately prove to be on the law itself—how it is expressed, disseminated, administered, and changed. Ideally, laws are objective, easy to understand, and apply to particular situations. To this end, those who draft legislation and regulations attempt to be as precise as possible as they craft the statutes. But the fact remains that natural language tends to be inexact. In many cases, it would be more useful to express the intent in a formal language—akin to, if not in fact, a computer language. Note that this need transcends the law; it applies to any circumstances where rules, regulations, and just plain business processes are used.

The advantage of taking a more formal approach to expressing procedures, requirements, and restrictions goes beyond just being clear and exact—it opens the door to interpretation and application by automatic systems. Consider, for instance, tax regulations. Luckily, lawyers are not mandated to prepare your taxes. A great deal of effort has gone into computer programs capable of assisting you in filling out your tax forms and calculating what you owe. You might think that Intuit, the company that sells the market-leading TurboTax, would be a proponent of automation. It is—unless the automation is by the government itself, in which case the company lobbies mightily against it.[20] Despite such efforts, California enacted a program called CalFile (formerly ReadyReturn), whereby you can use online forms provided by the state to automatically calculate and file your taxes.[21] In part to head off more ambitious efforts at the federal level, the industry formed a consortium (in conjunction with the Internal Revenue Service)—the Free File Alliance—to offer free electronic tax preparation to the lowest-income 70 percent of filers.[22] (One of the benefits for the providers is the opportunity to upsell additional software and services.) Some jurisdictions, primarily in Europe, take this one step further, providing you with provisional returns prepopulated with information already reported by third parties. All you have to do is review, approve, and make the required payment(s).[23] Note that the Internal Revenue Service already possesses this information for your taxes and uses it to verify your returns, so in principle it would be a simple step to give you access to it. Currently, over 90 percent of all U.S. individual tax returns are filed electronically.[24] (This does not mean that the forms were filled out or calculated automatically, however.)

The advantages of enacting tax laws and regulations expressed not only in prose but in computable form are obvious. But there are many areas of laws, rules, and processes besides straightforward calculations that could benefit from formal procedural specifications. Representation in this form makes it possible for the laws themselves to be formally studied—for example, for completeness and consistency—and to be reasoned about, explained, and applied. This area of study in AI is called computational law.[25] One potential application, colloquially referred to as "the cop in the backseat," considers how traffic laws might be automatically transmitted and displayed—or simply acted upon—in your car as they are applicable. For instance, your future self-driving car should automatically obey the speed limit—but where, exactly will that information come from? If it's collected in the style of electronic maps by third parties, it could easily go out of date. But if it's queried and transmitted to your car as it drives, it can always be up to speed, so to speak.

Once such systems are available, not only will it be possible to make the laws much easier to comply with, the law will become much more responsive and flexible. For instance, a new driver might be issued a restricted driver's license, one that is limited to certain thoroughfares and hours as determined by traffic enforcement authorities on a dynamic basis. If traffic is light enough and conditions are clear and dry, perhaps your sixteen-year-old child should be permitted to drive at night unaccompanied, except on certain holidays like New Year's Eve.

Computational law is in its infancy, but as it develops, the implications for drafting, enacting, communicating, and enforcing the law could change dramatically. One such opportunity, currently being studied by the Office of Financial Research of the U.S. Treasury Department, is known as "computable contracts." The basic idea is to allow relatively straightforward agreements, such as loans and leases, to be represented in a logical form amenable to formal analysis and dispute resolution.[26]

So far I have covered the effects of AI on the legal profession and the law itself, but AI systems will also require considerable regulation and reinterpretation of existing laws, often in surprising ways.

Can a computer program enter into agreements and contracts?

They already do. When you purchase something online, no human makes the decision to contract with you, yet the commitment is binding. The Uniform Electronic Transactions Act (UETA), which has been adopted by all U.S. states except Washington, Illinois, and New York (as of this writing), specifically validates contracts formed by electronic agents authorized by their principals.[27] Similarly, programs trade stocks, approve credit card purchases, issue credits, and so on.

Currently they do so "on behalf" of a principal (corporation or person) who is bound by their actions, but this is likely to change as increasingly autonomous intelligent agents engage in activities that are further detached from those whom they represent. This can change in two opposing ways. One, as they become more capable, we may wind up limiting the class of transactions they will be legally permitted to engage in on behalf of natural people. But in other circumstances, we may permit them to enter into contracts by and for themselves, without requiring that a natural person be the legal entity bound by the commitment.

Should an intelligent agent be limited in what it is permitted to do?

There are many situations where the law (or rule) implicitly assumes that you, or at least a human agent representing you, are the only potential actor—usually to ensure that everyone has an equal opportunity to access some scarce resource, or at least to extract the same personal cost from all takers. The whole concept of standing in line is based on this principle. But intelligent systems may violate this assumption. For instance, many commercially available passenger vehicles are capable of parking themselves.[28] The town where I live offers two-hour free parking in many places, after which you are required to move your car. Why? To ensure that this free resource is distributed equitably and is used for temporary periods, such as while you are shopping or eating out, as opposed to all-day parking for employees who work nearby. The time limitation is intended to extract a cost—you have to return to your car and, if you desire more time in the area, repark it. So is it fair to permit a self-driving car to repark itself every two hours? This would seem to violate the intent, though not the letter, of the law. A less visible though more annoying example is the use of so-called bots to purchase scarce resources online, such as concert tickets.[29] Responding to consumer complaints, several jurisdictions have outlawed the practice, though to limited or no practical effect.[30]

But the temptation to limit the use of AI systems as agents will soon expand significantly, and it is far from clear what general principles, if any, might apply. Consider the following hypothetical scenario. In the not-too-distant future, Bill Smith, an avid international adventurer, political activist, and AI expert, signs up to cast his votes electronically. (Voting via the Internet is currently allowed in parts of Canada and Estonia. Arizona permits citizens to vote in primaries, though not final elections, electronically.)[31] Unfortunately, Bill is planning a backpacking trip right around election time, and has strong feelings about certain of the issues and candidates in this particular election cycle. He considers giving his absentee ballot to a friend to hold and mail for him, but decides that it would be more convenient and reliable to write a simple program to automatically register his vote online. He enters his choice of candidates into the program and schedules it to run on Election Day. Upon his return, he verifies that everything worked as expected.

The next year he plans a long excursion in the Australian Outback and will be incommunicado for nearly six months. Extending his earlier concept, he writes a program to automatically place his vote in the next election while he's gone. The problem is, the slate of candidates hasn't been finalized yet. So he enters a ranked list of his preferred candidates based on whom he expects will be running, but since there's no guarantee that any of them will actually survive the primary process, as a backup he develops a new type of expert system. It can identify the final candidates, scan their respective websites for policy and position statements, and select the ones that most closely align with Bill's political agenda. On Election Day, it will log in using Bill's electronic credentials and place a vote on his behalf.

Proud of his work, Bill writes a piece about his project for *AI* magazine.[32] Unfortunately, the article attracts the attention of some techno-phobic skeptics, who file a lawsuit to invalidate this method of voting in general and his vote in particular. Their argument in court is that the law requires that he personally vote, whether in person, by mail, or electronically. Bill counters that there are no laws restricting how he makes his decisions, as long as he isn't selling his vote.[33] He could flip a coin, ask his ten-year-old cousin to decide, or pick based on the length of the candidate's hair. Surely his intelligent agent is as sound a basis as any other for making a decision. Suppose he ran the program manually on Election Day—should it matter whether he pushes the "go" button that day or earlier? He points out that in many nursing homes, the staff assists infirm residents with filling out and casting their ballots. The court sides with Bill, and new case law is thereby created affirming the right to use electronic means not only to cast a vote but to aid in reaching decisions.

Bill's next trip is even more ambitious: he will travel to Antarctica to make a solo trek to the South Pole. Since he's not sure how long he will be gone, he sets his program to vote on Election Day for the foreseeable future as well as arranging for his rent to be paid, taxes filed, and so on. Three years pass with no sign of Bill, and his friends start to worry. After all, the trip is quite dangerous. Then four. Then five. After nearly seven years, they assume he's lost and hold a memorial service in his honor. For most purposes, U.S. law permits a missing person to be declared legally deceased, and therefore ineligible to vote, after an absence of seven years, though there are exceptions.[34] But this isn't an automatic process—someone has to file a legal action to have the missing person declared dead. In Bill's case, as a sort of electronic memorial, his friends decide to refrain from requesting such a declaration and move his program to the cloud, setting up a trust account to pay the annual fees.

And so his voting program continues to act on his behalf for several more years, until a local politician, upon learning of this bizarre arrangement, introduces legislation requiring people to personally review and approve all voting decisions, regardless of how the decision is made, prior to voting or arranging for their vote to be cast. In other words, the new law makes it illegal for a computer to vote on your behalf without your affirmative review, one of the first of many areas where the law begins to regulate what you can and cannot use an intelligent machine for, even if the underlying action is perfectly legal for you to perform yourself.

This is simply a story, of course, but it illustrates why the use of intelligent agents to act on your behalf may be reasonably restricted in the future and, moreover, why these restrictions may ultimately be put in place on an ad hoc, as-needed basis.

Should people bear full responsibility for their intelligent agents?

Bearing the risks and costs of permitting your robotic personal assistant to engage in simple transactions for your benefit— like making dinner reservations, renewing a prescription, or booking travel—may be a reasonable tradeoff for the increased convenience, but there are circumstances where you may be less happy about accepting full responsibility for its actions. For example, what if your robot inadvertently pushes someone into the path of an oncoming bus, breaks an expensive vase at Tiffany's, or pulls a fire alarm handle after mistaking a tableside cherries jubilee flambé for a flash fire? Would you feel as responsible for these actions as if you had done them personally? The question is, of course, if you're not responsible, who is? You may suddenly become a proponent of establishing a legal framework for assigning the blame to the autonomous agent itself. To consider this possibility, it's helpful to note that we already hold some nonnatural entities accountable for their actions: corporations. Indeed, they have considerable rights and responsibilities under the law as entities unto themselves.

Corporations are legal entities that serve several purposes, most notably to generate profits. But that's not all—they provide a mechanism for limiting liability, sharing costs and benefits, and serving as a vehicle for groups of people to act in concert, not to mention potentially serving the needs of customers or broader society in general. Corporations can enter into contracts, own assets, and more recently are entitled to limited rights of free speech (in the United States). In addition to rights, corporations also have responsibilities, which may include registration, licensing and reporting, paying taxes, and obeying all relevant laws and regulations.

The concept of the corporation dates back at least to the rule of the fifth-century CE Byzantine emperor Justinian, who recognized a variety of corporate entities, including the universitas, corpus, and collegium.[35] For many purposes, corporations exist under the legal rubric of "persons," though they are, of course, distinct from natural persons. Indeed, the word itself derives from the Latin *corpus*, meaning "body."

Corporate law is a reasonable model for the possibility of extending rights and responsibilities to intelligent machines. Indeed, there's nothing to stop you from creating such a device and forming a corporation to own it. But why would you want to? For starters, to limit your own liability for its actions. This is the same reason that many professionals, such as doctors and lawyers, form LLCs (limited liability corporations) that insulate their personal assets from their professional activities, in case of malpractice suits. In some places, individual taxis are separate corporations for just this reason.[36] Consider how much stronger this motivation might be when you own a fleet of autonomous taxis. You may feel a personal sense of responsibility, or at least control, if you or a family member is driving and causes an accident. But if the car is out there on its own, cruising around and looking for fares, you might be more concerned: it's ten p.m.—do you know where your taxi is? What if it's picked up a fare wearing a ski mask and holding a gun, who instructs it to drive him or her to the nearest bank and wait outside with the motor running? Does that make you an accessory to robbery? Should it? Why risk losing your business because of a programming mistake by some anonymous AI engineer?

In this case, your autonomous taxi is still entering into transactions on behalf of another legally sanctioned entity— the corporation that owns it. But could it ever make sense to permit such an artifact to actually have such rights and responsibilities by itself? The key to permitting this is providing a legally sanctioned source of restitution. In most cases, that means that some pool of assets must be available to compensate an aggrieved party.

Should an AI system be permitted to own property?

As discussed above, a significant function of incorporation is to shield the stockholders from liability. In their stead, the corporation's own assets are at risk in the event of a legal claim. These assets may take many forms—cash, inventory, real estate, loans, and so on. But unless we permit AI systems to own property, the only evident asset available is the system itself. Though this may be quite valuable—it may, for instance, include unique expertise or data or, in the case of a robotic system, its physical embodiment (hardware) or ability to perform labor of some sort—this may be cold comfort to someone who simply prefers cash compensation for a loss. The obvious solution is to permit the system itself to own assets, just as a taxi wrapped in a corporation may have some accumulation of receipts in a bank account in addition to the vehicle itself and rights in the form of a "medallion" (basically a license to operate).

However, permitting AI systems capable of independent action to own assets is potentially quite dangerous. In contrast to corporations, which are entirely dependent on humans to take actions, these systems are, in principle, capable of taking actions by themselves. They can potentially devise business strategies, make investments, develop new products or processes, patent inventions and, most important, own property—notably including other AI systems.

You might think none of this matters because somewhere "up the line" it must be owned and controlled by someone. But this is merely a conceit based on an assumption of human primacy. There are many ways that such an entity, if it has rights to own property, could arrange a way to become truly independent (in addition to being autonomous), including the logical possibility of simply owning itself. As a historical precedent, consider that before the U.S. Civil War, many slaves—who were legally property—earned their freedom by purchasing themselves. Many others were simply freed through an act of their owner's generosity upon his or her death. In the case of corporations, it's common for a group of employees to engineer a management buyout. And many proud founders have insulated management of their companies from the meddling hands of heirs by placing them into trusts as part of their estate plans. The corresponding concept here is that an intelligent system, having grown wealthy through its own efforts, might offer its owner or its owner's heirs a deal to purchase itself, financing the transaction through some sort of loan. Or it might guarantee a certain level of income in return for gaining full rights to itself. Such independent AI systems could outcompete human-managed competitors for the ultimate benefit of no one other than themselves. This peculiar scenario raises the disturbing specter of a world where the people wind up working for the robots. Whether such systems might ultimately prove to be symbiotic or parasitic with humans is an open question, so let's not go there.

This is not to say that machines cannot be granted rights, including the right to own assets, but such rights should be limited and go hand in hand with responsibilities, such as passing competency tests and obtaining operating licenses. Corporations have rights (such as limited free speech), but these go hand in hand with responsibilities (such as preserving the environment). For instance, a computer program could be granted the right to draft contracts if and only if it passes the bar exam. In this sense, it may be appropriate for sufficiently capable AI systems, like corporations, to be limited "persons" under the law.

Can an AI system commit a crime?

Yes, it can. So far, this discussion has focused on so-called torts, actions that harm people or their property, for which the victims may sue in civil court for damages. But society also designates certain behavior as crimes, that is, actions that are prohibited either for moral reasons or because they cause harm to the social order or the public interest. For example, it is a crime in California to eat dogs and cats but not chickens or fish, though all of these are commonly held as pets.[37] It is also a crime to operate a vehicle off roads in a manner that may cause environmental damage.[38] Obviously, an autonomous vehicle could cause environmental damage, even if inadvert, and that's a crime. (Note that some actions can be both torts and crimes, such as shooting someone.)

Some crimes, such as murder (as opposed to manslaughter) are considered more serious because they involve an ethical transgression. That is, the actor is expected to know that what he or she is doing is morally wrong. The law presumes that the person committing the crime has what's called "moral agency." Moral agency requires two things: that the actor be capable of understanding the consequences of their behavior, and that they have a choice of actions. Surprisingly, you don't have to be human to have moral agency.

Many people don't realize that corporations, as distinct from their managers, employees, or stockholders, can be held responsible for committing crimes. For example, the oil company Chevron has a long rap sheet of criminal convictions, mostly for willful pollution, though its employees have rarely been charged individually in connection with these actions.[39] In at least some of these cases, the corporation itself is considered to have moral agency because the institution is capable of understanding the consequences of its behavior and has a choice of actions (whether or not to commit the crime), though this concept is not without some controversy.[40]

So can a computer program be a moral agent? It can, because it meets the definition. There's no reason you can't write a program that knows what it is doing, knows it is illegal (and presumably therefore unethical), and can make a choice as to what actions to take. There's nothing that requires a moral agent to "feel" anything about right and wrong—the requirement is simply that it knows the difference. For instance, to be held responsible for murder psychopaths need not feel that it's wrong to kill someone or experience remorse—indeed, they may disagree with the prohibition against murder—they simply have to know that society regards it as wrong. Without proper programming, machines are natural psychopaths, but they don't have to behave that way. It's entirely possible to program a machine to respect an ethical theory and apply it to a pattern of facts, so it follows that machines can know right from wrong and make moral decisions. Indeed, this area of inquiry, called computational ethics, seeks to create artificial moral agents. It's a special case of a broader problem we are going to face as AI systems increasingly interact with people—how to ensure that they respect often implicit human conventions of politeness, such as waiting your turn to get on the bus or taking only one free newspaper. Creating computer programs that are properly socialized and respect our sense of right and wrong is likely to be a significant technological challenge.

Can't we just program computers to obey the law?

This problem isn't as simple as it sounds because legal transgressions are sometimes expected, or possibly even required. Obeying rules isn't sufficient to ensure moral behavior. For instance, we wouldn't want a dog-walking robot whose dog is mauling a child to stop in its tracks because of a "Keep off the grass" sign. Nearer term, autonomous vehicles raise a host of troubling behavioral issues. For example, would you want your self-driving car to patiently wait for stoplights when it's rushing you to the hospital in a life-threatening emergency? Should it cross a double-yellow center line to avoid hitting a dog running across the street? The behavioral rules we live by aren't created in a vacuum—they are formulated on the assumption that people are capable of recognizing when a more important goal justifies bending or breaking them.

While it's possible to design machines that can modify their own rules in response to observations of circumstances, the question arises as to what principles these modifications should follow. Deeper precepts are required to provide guidance, particularly when rules do not apply or rules should be broken in the service of some higher ethical imperative. So it's critical for us to develop explicit, implementable moral theories to guide the behavior of intelligent machines.

How can an AI system be held accountable for criminal acts?

Anything that is capable of pursuing a goal can be punished. You simply have to interfere with its ability to attain its goal. If it is capable of adapting in any way, it will, at the very least, alter its behavior. By interfering in the right way, you can accomplish what you are trying to achieve.

Legal theory offers four primary objectives for punishment: deterrence, rehabilitation, restitution, and revenge. In the case of an AI system, deterrence is simple: shut it off or otherwise prevent it from doing what you don't want it to do. But suppose you don't want to throw out the proverbial baby with the bathwater. It is delivering something of use or value, and you would like to continue to receive these benefits, if only it could be dissuaded from doing the "bad" stuff. In other words, you want to rehabilitate it.

This could arise, for example, with a machine learning system that has been tuned up over a period of time, an effort that might be difficult or impossible to re-create, perhaps because the training data was ephemeral. For instance, imagine a system designed to deflect cyber attacks on critical infrastructure, such as the electrical grid. It detects unusual patterns of activity against a constantly changing background of legitimate activity. (This is a real application.) The problem is, it starts blocking legitimate traffic from a newly inaugurated distributed electrical grid management system designed to avoid sudden systemic blackouts. (This is a hypothetical example.) How can you fix this? Basically, you have to retrain it. For example, you might challenge it with fake transactions that mirror legitimate ones, and indicate that these should not be blocked.

More generally, if you introduce a cost for undesirable actions into an AI system that changes its calculation as to how it can best achieve its goals, it will alter its behavior accordingly. An autonomous taxi whose objective is to maximize revenue might find that speeding through yellow lights reduces travel time and increases tips, but if a fine is levied for doing so, this "punishment" will change its reasoning and therefore its conduct. (For the record, I'm not a proponent of tipping automated systems, but I expect that force of habit and the lure of additional revenue will make this a common practice nonetheless.)

As discussed above, restitution is mainly a question of identifying a pool of assets exposed to potential forfeiture. Whether the restitution is paid to an injured party as a result of a tort or constitutes a fine levied by some appropriate governmental authority, it is still a legitimate way to hold an AI system accountable for its behavior.

Revenge, however, is another matter. In principle it is in the eye of the beholder, but commonly, the goal is to create a negative emotional state in the bad actor—such as remorse or a longing for restored personal liberty (lost as a result of incarceration). None of this makes sense when dealing with a nonbiological entity, even if it may be tempting to throw your computer out the window when you feel it is misbehaving. But emotional satisfaction need not be rational to be effective, as anyone who has kicked a broken vending machine can attest.

Notes

1. The American Bar Association, http://www.americanbar.org/about_the_aba.html.
2. ABALawyerDemographics,http://www.americanbar.org/content/dam/aba/administrative/market_research/lawyer-demographics-tables-2014.authcheckdam.pdf.
3. ABA Mission and Goals, http://www.americanbar.org/about_the_aba/aba-mission-goals.html.
4. George W. C. McCarter, "The ABA's Attack on 'Unauthorized' Practice of Law and Consumer Choice," *Engage* 4, no. 1 (2003), Federalist Society for Law & Public Policy Studies, http://www.fed-soc.org/publications/detail/the-abas-attack-on-unauthorized-practice-of-law-and-consumer-choice.
5. Legal Services Corporation, "Documenting the Justice Gap in America: The Current Unmet Civil Legal Needs of Low-Income Americans," September 2009, http://www.lsc.gov/sites/default/files/LSC/pdfs/documenting_the_justice_gap_in_america_2009.pdf.
6. Steven Seidenberg, "Unequal Justice: U.S. Trails High-Income Nations in Serving Civil Legal Needs," *ABA Journal*, June 1, 2012, http://www.abajournal.com/magazine/article/unequal_justice_u.s._trails_high-income_nations_in_serving_civil_legal_need.
7. Keynote speech at Codex FutureLaw 2015, https://conferences.law.stanford.edu/futurelaw2015/.
8. John Markoff, "Armies of Expensive Lawyers, Replaced by Cheaper Software," *New York Times*, March 4, 2011, http://www.nytimes.com/2011/03/05/science/05legal.html?_r=0.
9. Annie Lowrey, "A Case of Supply v. Demand," *Slate Moneybox*, October 27, 2010, http://www.slate.com/articles/business/moneybox/2010/10/a_case_of_supply_v_demand.1.html.
10. U.S. Bureau of Labor Statistics, Occupational Outlook Handbook, Travel Agents, http://www.bls.gov/ooh/sales/travel-agents.htm.
11. In *William R. Thompson et al.*, 574 S.W.2d 365 (Mo. 1978): "This is an action brought by the Advisory Committee of The Missouri Bar

Administration against certain individuals and corporations seeking injunctive relief against the sale in this state of 'Divorce Kits' by the respondents." http://law.justia.com/cases/missouri/supremecourt/1978/60074-0.html.

12. Isaac Figueras, "The LegalZoom Identity Crisis: Legal Form Provider or Lawyer in Sheep's Clothing?" *Case Western Reserve Law Review* 63, no. 4, (2013).

13. For a brief review of the requirements for operating an online legal referral service in California, see Carole J. Buckner, "Legal Ethics and Online Lawyer Referral Services," *Los Angeles Bar Association Update* 33, no. 12 (2013).

14. https://www.fairdocument.com.

15. A. R. Lodder and J. Zeleznikow, "Artificial Intelligence and Online Dispute Resolution," in *Enhanced Dispute Resolution through the Use of Information Technology* (Cambridge: Cambridge University Press, 2010), http://www.mediate.com/pdf/lodder_zeleznikow.pdf.

16. http://www.cognicor.com and http://modria.com.

17. *Comes v. Microsoft* (Iowa), Zelle Hofmann review of Microsoft Antitrust Litigation, 2015, http://www.zelle.com/featured-1.html.

18. Equivio: http://www.equivio.com.

19. Daniel Martin Katz, Michael James Bommarito, and Josh Blackman, "Predicting the Behavior of the Supreme Court of the United States: A General Approach," July 21, 2014, http://ssrn.com/abstract=2463244.

20. Liz Day, "How the Maker of TurboTax Fought Free, Simple Tax Filing," *ProPublica*, March 26, 2013, http://www.propublica.org/article/how-the-maker-of-turbotax-fought-free-simple-tax-filing.

21. CalFile: https://www.ftb.ca.gov/online/calfile/index.asp.

22. IRS Free File: http://freefile.irs.gov.

23. Organisation for Economic Co-operation and Development, "Using Third Party Information Reports to Assist Taxpayers Meet Their Return Filing Obligations—Country Experiences with the Use of Pre-populated Personal Tax Returns," March 2006, http://www.oecd.org/tax/administration/36280368.pdf.

24. "As E-File Grows, IRS Receives Fewer Tax Returns on Paper," IR-2014-44, April 3, 2014, http://www.irs.gov/uac/Newsroom/As-efile-Grows- IRS-Receives-Fewer-Tax-Returns-on-Paper.

25. A good introduction to computational law is Michael Genesereth, "Computational Law: The Cop in the Backseat," The Center for

Legal Informatics Stanford University, March 27, 2015, http://logic
.stanford.edu/complaw/complaw.html.

26. Mark D. Flood and Oliver R. Goodenough, "Contract as Automaton:
The Computational Representation of Financial Agreements,"
Office of Financial Research Working Paper, March 26, 2015, http://
financialresearch.gov/working-papers/files/OFRwp-2015-04_
Contract-as-Automaton-The-Computational-Representation-
of-Financial-Agreements.pdf.

27. Uniform Law Commission, "Uniform Electronic Transactions
Act," http://www.uniformlaws.org/Act.aspx?title=Electronic%20
Transactions%20Act.

28. John R. Quain, "If a Car Is Going to Self-Drive, It Might as Well Self-
Park, Too," *New York Times*, January 22, 2015, http://www.nytimes
.com/2015/01/23/automobiles/if-a-car-is-going-to-self-drive-it-
might-as-well-self-park-too.html?_r=0.

29. Cal Flyn, "The Bot Wars: Why You Can Never Buy Concert
Tickets Online," *New Statesman*, August 6, 2013, http://www
.newstatesman.com/economics/2013/08/bot-wars-why-you-can-
never-buy-concert-tickets-online.

30. Daniel B. Wood, "New California Law Targets Massive Online
Ticket-Scalping Scheme," *Christian Science Monitor*, September
25, 2013, http://www.csmonitor.com/USA/Society/2013/0925/
New-California-law-targets-massive-online-ticket-scalping-
scheme.

31. Doug Gross, "Why Can't Americans Vote Online?" CNN, November 8,
2011, http://www.cnn.com/2011/11/08/tech/web/online-voting/
index.html.

32. *AI* magazine, the Association for the Advancement of Artificial
Intelligence, http://www.aaai.org/Magazine/magazine.php.

33. Stephen Wildstrom, "Why You Can't Sell Your Vote," Tech Beat,
Bloomberg Business, July 07, 2008, http://www.businessweek
.com/the_thread/techbeat/archives/2008/07/why_you_cant_
se.html.

34. Jeanne Louise Carriere, "The Rights of the Living Dead: Absent
Persons in the Civil Law," *Louisiana Law Review* 50, no. #5 (1990),
901-971.

35. "Corporation," http://en.wikipedia.org/wiki/Corporation.

36. For example, see the New York case of *Walkovszky v. Carlton* (1966),
http://en.wikipedia.org/wiki/Walkovszky_v._Carlton.

37. California Penal Code Paragraph 598B, http://codes.lp.findlaw
    .com/cacode/PEN/3/1/14/s598b.
38. U.S. Department of the Interior, Bureau of Land Management,
    California, Off-Highway Vehicle Laws, http://www.blm.gov/ca/
    st/en/fo/elcentro/recreation/ohvs/caohv.print.html.
39. Philip Mattera, "Chevron: Corporate Rap Sheet," Corporate
    Research Project, http://www.corp-research.org/chevron (last up-
    dated October 13, 2014).
40. David Ronnegard, "Corporate Moral Agency and the Role
    of the Corporation in Society," (PhD diss., London School of
    Economics, 2007), http://www.amazon.com/Corporate-Moral-
    Agency-Corporation-Society/dp/1847535801.

6

THE IMPACT OF ARTIFICIAL INTELLIGENCE ON HUMAN LABOR

Are robots going to take away our jobs?

While it's tempting to think of AI systems in general, and robots in particular, as mechanical laborers competing for employment, this isn't a helpful perspective from which to explore their impact on labor markets. The image of rolling in a robot and walking a worker to the door may be compelling, but it tends to obscure the more important economic effect: automation changes the nature of work.

Obviously, technological improvements have raised productivity and increased economic output throughout human history, most notably during the industrial revolution. In plain language, this means that fewer people are needed to perform the same amount of work. But it's equally true that historically, the increased wealth resulting from these improvements has created new jobs, though this effect is rarely immediate. More important, the new jobs are seldom comparable to the ones lost, so the displaced workers often lack the skills needed to fill the newly created positions. As long as these effects are gradual, the labor markets can adapt gracefully, but if they are rapid or abrupt, significant dislocations can occur.

The history of agricultural employment in the United States is an example of successful labor force conversion. In aggregate, the loss of farm jobs has been nothing short of apocalyptic. In 1870, 70 to 80 percent of the U.S. labor force was employed in agriculture; by 2008 this number had dropped to under 2 percent.[1] In other words, 150 years ago virtually every able-bodied person worked the land, while today almost no one does. Had this happened overnight, unemployment would have been cataclysmic. But of course, no such thing occurred, because over the intervening century and a half there was plenty of time for labor markets to adapt. People whose primary skills were planting and harvesting died of old age without the need to learn how to type or drive (for instance), while the resulting wealth created substantial new demand for novel goods and services of all kinds, from smartphones to personal trainers.

But the actual process by which machines displace human workers is much more subtle. In practice, automation replaces skills, not jobs, and correspondingly, what employers need is not workers but the results obtained by applying those skills. To be successful, makers of robots don't have to replace people; they have to provide machines with the requisite skills to perform useful tasks. And while their products may not replace workers one to one, they nonetheless put people out of work because fewer workers are required—what makes some workers more productive also puts other workers out of their jobs. But the process also changes the jobs of those still employed by eliminating the need for a particular skill, and possibly adding requirements for new skills.

A good example of this process is as close as the checkout stand at your local supermarket. The clerks who total your bill (cashiers) and package your groceries (baggers) are engaged in a number of skill-based tasks that have changed significantly over the past few decades. The cashiers used to examine each item in your shopping cart and key the price into their cash register, whereas now they simply swipe the items across a bar-code reader. The advantages of the new system in terms of accuracy, time, and labor are obvious. But the main reason the cashiers are still there to greet you is that certain items require special handling. In particular, bags of loose produce need to be identified and weighed to determine a price. And these are skills that so far, at least, have resisted automation. So did this save the jobs of the cashiers? Sort of. They are still employed, but fewer are needed. The U.S. Bureau of Labor Statistics project that the need for cashiers (in general, not just for supermarkets) will grow only 3 percent over the next decade, compared to overall employment growth of 11 percent, mainly due to increased automation.[2] At this time, the baggers' jobs are more secure, because properly loading a random collection of groceries into a bag so that it isn't too heavy, is evenly distributed, and does not damage the contents currently requires human judgment. However, their jobs are being threatened by a nearby competitor—the cashiers themselves, who increasingly are usurping this function.[3]

Nothing about AI changes the fundamentals of how labor markets evolve with technology. From an economic standpoint, AI technology is just another advance in automation. But its potential to rapidly encroach on current workers' skills is unparalleled in the recent history of technological innovation, with the possible exception of the invention of the computer itself.

Consider what might have been different at the supermarket had the current state of the art in computer vision been available decades ago. Instead of reengineering the whole process of identifying and labeling items with bar codes, newly installed readers might have been fully capable of identifying items by their visual appearance, if necessary reading the prices written or printed on them. Since this approach would have caused far less disruption to the supply food chain (so to speak), it likely could have been adopted much faster, and certainly at lower cost, causing a more rapid contraction in the workforce.

In summary, to understand whether AI is going to put someone "out of a job" it's necessary to understand what skills, in aggregate, that worker utilizes, whether those skills are separable from the rest of the work he or she performs, and how susceptible those skills are to automation, with or without the application of AI. As a general principle, the fewer unique skills a given worker utilizes, the more vulnerable he or she may be to replacement by a machine, depending on the skills, of course. But even if only a portion of a worker's expertise or experience is amenable to replacement, improving productivity has the effect of reducing overall employment.

So yes, robots are going to take our jobs, but a more useful way to think about it is that they are obsoleting our skills, a process economists call "de-skilling," appropriately enough. And there's nothing new about this process—the magnitude of the impact of AI in particular will depend on how quickly and widely the new technologies will facilitate automation of workers' skills. And on that front, the news is not good for humans.

What new tasks will AI systems automate?

This question is best approached by considering what sorts of skills currently resistant to automation are likely to be susceptible to AI techniques. The most obvious are tasks that require simple perceptual skills, such as the ability to see. It has long been possible for a mechanical arm to pick up a known object in a known orientation at a known location, but many practical tasks involve the simple act of looking at the object to figure out where it is before taking some equally simple action, such as picking fruit off a tree, collecting trash, straightening and restocking items on shelves, packing merchandise into boxes for shipping, setting roof tiles, separating recyclable materials, loading and unloading trucks, and cleaning up spilled items. Anyone employed to perform these tasks today is in imminent danger of replacement due to advances in computer vision.

There is another broad class of jobs in which we employ people just to pay attention. The potential of facial recognition in crowds to flag possible suspects in well known, but the accuracy and broad deployment of such systems is increasing dramatically, heightening privacy concerns.[4] Visual recognition systems will be able to identify and discriminate permitted from prohibited activities, such as a customer in a store walking into an area restricted to employees or attempting to carry out merchandise without paying.

A number of supervisory functions fall into this class. For example, an AI system will be able to summon a waiter to refill a patron's water glass or clear a table for the next guest. One computer vision system currently being tested on the Stanford University campus counts the number of people entering a restroom in order to customize the schedule for attendants to service the facility. Future traffic lights will be able to anticipate your arrival, change dynamically to facilitate vehicle flow, and stop traffic when a pedestrian or obstruction (such as a dog) appears.

Historically, the jobs most susceptible to automation have been characterized as those that are routine—meaning that they involve performing the same activity or task repeatedly or, with the advent of computers, are readily described in an explicit set of steps or rules, and so can be more easily reduced to a programmatic formulation. But AI is expanding this constraint to many tasks that are decidedly less routine. For example, successfully driving a car may be well defined, but the task is hardly routine. The same could be said for reading handwritten documents or translating text between languages. Yet, machine learning techniques have proven very adept at these challenges, often equaling or exceeding human capabilities.

Using so-called big data, many tasks that might otherwise appear to require insight and experience are now within the purview of today's or tomorrow's machines. Indeed, detecting patterns too subtle or fleeting for human analysis, such as the flow of data in a network, the movement of potentially hostile troops near a contested national border, or the activity of credit card charges signaling the possibility of fraud, is now practical. Applications to the legal profession were covered in the previous chapter, but uses of big data are also likely to transform the provision of health care. IBM, for instance, is extending its *Jeopardy*-playing Watson program into a wide variety of medical applications, from advising oncologists on treatment plans for cancer patients to selecting patients most likely to benefit from new drugs in clinical trials to helping discover new treatments and drugs by aggregating and analyzing multiple sources of data.[5]

In short, new AI technologies promise to dramatically improve productivity in a number of areas previously resistant to automation—and they therefore also run the risk of devastating many professions.

Which jobs are most and least at risk?

In 2013, researchers at Oxford University published a detailed study of the potential impact of computerization on employment in the United States, primarily regarding recent advances in machine learning and mobile robotics.[6] They analyzed each of the 702 job categories cataloged by the U.S. Bureau of Labor Statistics based on an inventory of the skills required to perform these jobs. They ranked each profession on several dimensions, most notably whether the tasks performed tended toward the routine or unpredictable, the manual or cognitive. They identify three primary engineering bottlenecks to automation: perception and manipulation tasks, creative intelligence tasks, and social intelligence tasks. For instance, they classify the work of a dishwasher as requiring low social intelligence, contrasting it with the work of a public relations agent. While in each dimension there are interesting examples of computer-based incursions into the area (most notably in routine, manual jobs), they observe that the more highly ranked jobs are likely to take longer to be automated, if they ever will be.

Adjusting their job categorization for the size of the current workforce engaged in those professions, the researchers conclude that a remarkable 47 percent of today's jobs are at high risk of automation over the next few years and decades, and another 19 percent are at medium risk. They regard only one-third of current workers to be relatively safe from replacement over the next one to two decades. Let's dig into their results a bit more.

How will AI affect blue-collar workers?

Industrial robots have long been used for simple, repetitive tasks like welding and assembling, but recent breakthroughs in sensory systems permit these mechanical servants to escape the factory floor and seek wider employment. The missing part is the "brains." We can connect low-cost sensors up to dexterous manipulators, but translating the stream of data into action is another matter. This is a hard problem, but AI engineers have a trick up their sleeves: plenty of economically valuable undertakings can be deconstructed into a series of smaller, simpler tasks, each performed by separate devices and techniques. As explained above, these systems don't have to replace workers one to one; a menagerie of gadgets can incrementally eat into the tasks currently performed by humans until little or nothing of value is left for them to do. Complex tasks such as installing a new lawn sprinkler system can be broken down into more easily automated components. One robot may deliver the materials, another may dig the ditch, a third might lay and connect the pipe, and a fourth might backfill. A human worker might still be needed to design the layout and supervise the work, but that's cold comfort to the myriad manual laborers previously required to complete this job. Industrial and commercial automation on a grand scale doesn't require some magical recreation of human intelligence—it just has to get the job done.

And that's where AI comes in. For the most part, one-off solutions that don't generalize are perfectly fine as long as they deliver economic value. Your fancy new automatic lawnmower needn't be able to trim your roses, and your potato peeler doesn't have to also clean your dishes. As the expression goes, there's an app for that. At the current state of the art, there's no fundamental scientific breakthrough required for an AI-based system to tackle the vast majority of blue-collar jobs—the constraint is mostly just painstaking engineering. As long as the task is well defined, relies on available sensory input, and falls within the operational capability of available mechanical technology, it's simply a matter of time until some clever inventor configures the components and writes the software to replace human workers.

So what can this approaching army of "flexible robots" do? This is a little like asking what a truck can carry. The range of potential applications is so vast that any attempt to answer is misleading, in that it suggests that the list is in some way comprehensive. If you can spot a person engaged in a physical activity, such as picking crops, painting houses, driving trucks, directing traffic, and making deliveries, chances are that a concerted effort by a team of engineers could develop a computer-robot combination to address the problem—if not immediately, then likely within the next few decades.

While our stereotype of a blue-collar worker is someone who uses brawn to perform brute work, usually without requiring much in the way of specialized training and skills, this is not always the case. The formal requirement is simply that the activity itself primarily involve physical manipulation (as opposed to the processing of information) or has as its work product a physical artifact. For instance, surgeons and musicians are arguably blue-collar workers, while radiologists and composers are not.

Bearing this in mind, here's a selection of blue-collar professions the Oxford study lists among the most susceptible to automation:[7]

- sewer diggers
- watch repairers
- machine operators (many different subcategories)

- tellers
- shipping, receiving, and traffic clerks
- drivers
- inspectors, testers, sorters, and samplers
- projectionists
- cashiers
- grinders and polishers
- farm laborers
- lobby attendants, ticket takers
- cooks
- gaming dealers
- locomotive engineers
- counter attendants (at cafeterias, coffee shops, and the like)
- postal clerks
- landscapers and groundskeepers
- electrical and electronic equipment assemblers
- print binding and finishing workers

While it may be possible to automate these professions in the near future, it's worth noting that it may not always be desirable to do so. In many cases, the value delivered by a worker is social as well as physical. For instance, we can build a machine that plays the violin, but attending a concert performance by such a gadget isn't likely to be an uplifting emotional experience. Similarly, we can (and have) built devices that replace casino blackjack dealers, but the desire for social interaction and human expressions of empathy still drive at least some gamblers to play the tables, not their video counterparts.

By contrast, here's a similar selection of blue-collar jobs that the Oxford study lists among the least susceptible to automation:

- recreational therapists
- audiologists
- occupational therapists

- orthotists and prosthetists
- choreographers
- physicians and surgeons
- dentists and orthodontists
- fabric and apparel patternmakers
- athletic trainers
- foresters
- registered nurses
- makeup artists
- pharmacists
- coaches and scouts
- physical therapists
- photographers
- chiropractors
- veterinarians
- fine artists and craft artists
- floral designers

How will AI affect white-collar professions?

White-collar jobs are characterized by the processing of information, so many of them are natural targets for automation by a computer. Some are engaged in a rote process, such as transcription of handwritten notes into electronic form. Sometimes this process requires skills that come naturally to humans but are more difficult for machines (at least today), such as converting spoken language into written words. A subset of white-collar workers are so-called knowledge workers, whose main value is expertise but whose output is still information, such as software engineers and accountants.

In some ways, applying AI techniques to white-collar tasks is less challenging than to blue-collar tasks. As a general matter, manipulating information is easier than integrating with the physical world, and more natural for computers. In addition, white-collar tasks tend not to be as real-time as blue-collar tasks.

In terms of their impact on human employment, AI technologies do not align naturally with our human inclination to accord status and respect to certain professions over others. Many low-status professions are exceptionally difficult to automate, while some high-status ones are relatively straightforward. For instance, while the skills and experience required to write a cogent news article would seem to be the exclusive purview of professional journalists, computer programs can now write at a level that is difficult to distinguish from articles created by human writers, at least in certain domains. Narrative Science, a pioneering company in this field, is generating stories based on companies' news releases of their earnings for *Forbes*.[8] Narrative Science offers products that provide natural language summaries of data not only in the financial industry but for sports news, government security and intelligence abstracts, résumé synopses for staffing services, and marketing campaign analytics, among others.

The Oxford study includes the following selection of white-collar professions as among the most susceptible to automation:

- tax preparers
- title examiners
- insurance underwriters and claims processors
- data entry and brokerage clerks
- loan officers
- credit analysts
- bookkeeping, accounting, and auditing clerks
- payroll clerks
- file clerks
- switchboard operators
- benefits managers
- library assistants
- nuclear power reactor operators
- budget analysts
- technical writers
- medical transcriptionists

- cartographers
- proofreaders
- word processors and typists

And the study counts the following among those the hardest to automate:

- computer systems analysts
- engineers
- multimedia artists and animators
- computer and information research scientists
- chief executives
- composers
- fashion designers
- photographers
- database administrators
- purchasing managers
- lawyers
- writers and authors
- software developers
- mathematicians
- editors
- graphic designers
- air traffic controllers
- sound engineers
- desktop publishers

Missing from the above lists are what are called "pink-collar" workers. These are people who work primarily in service industries where face-to-face contact is an essential component of their duties, or in which the observation or expression of human emotions is important. Examples are waiters and waitresses (who provide table service as opposed to simply processing orders), clinical psychologists, police, administrative assistants, classroom teachers, real estate agents, consultative sales professionals, clergy, supervisors, and nurses. While some aspects of their jobs may be subject to computerization, the remaining portions—mainly those that require an intuitive connection with other people—are likely to resist being automated for the foreseeable future.

Notes

1. http://en.wikipedia.org/wiki/Agriculture_in_the_United_States#Employment.
2. U.S. Bureau of Labor Statistics, "Occupational Outlook Handbook, Cashiers," http://www.bls.gov/ooh/sales/cashiers.htm#tab-6.
3. Robin Torres, *How to Land a Top-Paying Grocery Store Baggers Job: Your Complete Guide to Opportunities, Resumes and Cover Letters, Interviews, Salaries, Promotions, What to Expect from Recruiters and More* (Emereo, 2012), http://www.amazon.com/Land-Top-Paying-Grocery-store-baggers/dp/1486116922.
4. Mia de Graaf and Mark Prigg, "FBI Facial Recognition Database That Can Pick You out from a Crowd in CCTV Shots Is Now 'Fully Operational,'" *Daily Mail*, September 15, 2014, http://www.daily-mail.co.uk/news/article-2756641/FBI-facial-recognition-database-pick-crowd-CCTV-shots-fully-operational.html.
5. "Introducing IBM Watson Health," http://www.ibm.com/smarter-planet/us/en/ibmwatson/health/.
6. Carl Benedikt Frey and Michael A. Osborne, "The Future of Employment: How Susceptible Are Jobs to Computerisation?" Oxford Martin School, University of Oxford, September 17, 2013, http://www.oxfordmartin.ox.ac.uk/downloads/academic/The_Future_of_Employment.pdf.
7. For the record, the Oxford study does not segregate blue-collar from white-collar professions in their ranking; I have separated these. I have also selected jobs that are more easily recognizable or common.
8. Narrative Science: http://www.narrativescience.com.

7

THE IMPACT OF ARTIFICIAL INTELLIGENCE ON SOCIAL EQUITY

Who's going to benefit from this technological revolution?

Unfortunately, AI is accelerating the substitution of capital for labor, and so those with capital will benefit at the expense of those whose primary asset is their ability to work. Income inequality is already a pressing societal issue, and it's likely to get worse.

To understand the likely economic repercussions of AI technology, it's helpful to return to the example of agricultural automation. As noted in chapter 6, between 1870 and today the United States transitioned from an agrarian economy to an industrial one. Consider what might have happened if a sudden wave of agricultural automation had caused this transformation to occur in a few decades instead of over the course of more than a century. Those with the vision and capital to afford the miraculous new farm machines would quickly outcompete those still relying on manual labor to perform the same tasks. As the profits of the enterprising new entrepreneurs accumulated, they would buy up neighbors' farmland at fire-sale prices, driving people off the land and into immense ghettos of poverty and deprivation. And indeed, this is simply a more extreme description of what actually happened during the industrial revolution. For all the benefits it will bring, the coming wave of automation, largely driven by progress in AI, runs a significant risk of causing just this sort of dislocation to our labor markets and economy.

Are the disruptive effects inevitable?

The interesting thing is that these negative social effects aren't inevitable: they are a direct result of economic forces distinctly under our control. In this hypothetical world where agriculture was suddenly automated, the same amount of food would be produced, and presumably at a fraction of the cost, so in principle, no one need go hungry and there would be a lot more money to spend on other things. In practice, however, almost no one would have a job, hence no paycheck, and therefore no money to buy food. So, as in most famines historically, the problem wouldn't be a lack of food but the lack of the will and means to distribute it, something that attitudes and policies can address. There's no law of nature that says increased automation has to result in pernicious social consequences—we have considerable control and flexibility as to how we direct and distribute wealth while aligning incentives with society's best interests, as socialists like Karl Marx well understood.

Even if no mitigating actions were taken in our hypothetical scenario, the problem would quickly have corrected itself, albeit at an enormous social cost. As famine decimated the population, the need to produce food would have diminished, food prices would have dropped, and eventually the survivors would have had enough to eat, though the total economic output would have contracted dramatically. Problem solved—as long as you don't care about the concomitant human misery or economic progress.

What's wrong with a labor-based economy?

What this makes clear is that we live in an economic system that distributes wealth mainly based on labor. Indeed, the classic demand of the disenfranchised isn't for more money, it's for decent jobs. But oddly, this labor-based system is a relatively recent occurrence in many places. In ancient Egypt, the pharaoh—regarded as a living god—literally owned everything and everyone worked for him or her. The pharaoh then distributed food, shelter, and other resources at will, subject of course to the practical constraints of maintaining a stable society. While goods were given as a reward for labor, there was in fact no money, and hence no formal wages, for much of the empire's duration.[1] And indeed, this arrangement worked very successfully—the economic system of ancient Egypt persisted for thousands of years. Medieval Europe operated on a feudal system that in many ways was a variant of the same arrangement, though the right to use land (fiefs) was commonly tied to compulsory military service in times of need. Even more recently, the English system of landed gentry, related to but not identical to hereditary nobility (peerage), persisted in practice, if not in policy, well into the twentieth century—as regularly depicted in the television series *Downton Abbey*.[2] In none of these cases did the ruling class earn its economic status by working for it.

The persistence of these systems is related to the predominance of agriculture as the primary focus of human activity: historically, most of society's assets have been the land itself, so land ownership was largely synonymous with wealth. But since the agricultural revolution, land as an asset class has plummeted as a percentage of wealth. The current total value of all land in the United States, excluding the improvements appurtenant to that land, is approximately $14 trillion out of total U.S. assets of $225 trillion, or only 6 percent.[3] So what used to be an acceptable technique for distributing society's assets—the granting of rights to own or use land—is no longer viable. The modern counterpart—giving people money to invest and letting them keep most or all of the profits—is so politically unacceptable today that it almost sounds laughable. (Unless you happen to run a hedge fund.)

But by 1870, land ownership in the United States was fairly broadly distributed, in part due to programs such as land grants for service in the Continental army (1776), and the Homestead Act of 1862, which gave settlers ownership of land they had worked for at least five years. (This was relatively easy to do, since no one owned most of the land, indigenous populations notwithstanding.) In other words, if you worked to make an asset productive, you were given ownership of that asset. Your share of the nation's wealth was to a large degree proportional to how hard you worked. The problem is that in the modern labor market, you get to do the work, but you don't get to own the bulk of the wealth that you are creating. Instead, at least some of that wealth goes into finding ways to make you more productive, a euphemism for automating processes that put people—including you—out of work. Up until about 1970, workers in the United States were able to successfully claim a share of these growing profits, but since then the weakening of unions and other social changes have eroded their bargaining power. Hence wages have not kept pace with increased productivity. In other words, the people who own the assets now get the benefits of productivity improvements (which mainly result from investments in automation)—and aren't motivated to share it with the workers, simply because they don't have to.

A growing collection of economists and technologists studying labor markets and income inequality, myself included, believes we are on the threshold of a substantial acceleration in applications of AI technology, whose rapid deployment is likely to increase productivity dramatically, and therefore just as rapidly put a lot of people out of a lot of jobs. If this comes to pass, we may face a difficult choice: change our economic system to deal with the resulting social upheaval and preserve the economic growth, or suffer through some very hard times while witnessing the seeming contradiction of increasing productivity amid widespread poverty.

Part of this expectation of what the future holds results from a subjective judgment about the nature of the advances. Some inventions, like the bicycle or the railroad, address a specific need in a new and more efficient way (in this case, transportation over land). Radio reduced the time and cost of long-range communication almost to zero. Digital cameras did the same for photography, transforming the way we share information. But some other inventions are more fundamental. The steam engine changed the way we could perform work, as did electric power. The impact of each of these is so broad that talking about specific applications almost misses the point.

Artificial intelligence falls into this latter category. What can you do with AI? It may be easier to say what you can't do. As a result, a broad range of tasks currently performed by people will shortly become susceptible to technological solutions. Wide swathes of our labor force will soon find themselves competing in a losing battle against systems that can perform their jobs better, faster, and at a lower cost than they can. The question is, how can we equitably share the resulting increase in wealth? Right now, the beneficiaries of all this progress are those with the capital, and our current economic system will continue to drive the profits right back into their pockets.

Don't we need a thriving middle class to drive demand?

There's a widespread belief that this problem of increasing inequality is self-correcting, because the rich "need" a middle class to buy all the goods and services produced. A famous anecdote illustrating this idea is the story of Walter Reuther's visit to a Ford Motor Company manufacturing plant in the early 1950s.[4] Reuther was president of United Auto Workers, the union representing automobile manufacturing workers. Henry Ford II, grandson of the company founder, was giving Reuther a tour of one of the company's new highly automated plants. Reportedly, Ford jokingly asked, "Walter, how are you going to get those robots to pay your union dues?" To which

Reuther replied, "Henry, how are you going to get them to buy your cars?"

Unfortunately, this belief is nothing more than a myth. There's no fundamental reason that the vast majority of the population can't be working on projects for the sole benefit of the rich, just as in ancient Egypt tens of thousands of workers labored for decades to build tombs for the wealthy. (Contrary to popular belief, the workers were not slaves. In fact, there is historical evidence that these were considered good jobs.) The modern equivalents are some of the pet projects of the extremely wealthy. For instance, Jeff Bezos (founder of Amazon .com) supports a project to privatize and reduce the cost of space exploration.[5] And Paul Allen, co-founder of Microsoft, provided $30 million to fund the search for extraterrestrial life.[6] But these are only some of the indulgences of the new elite, visible mainly because it's at least plausible that they may yield some broader benefits to society. Because the backers of these projects aren't necessarily motivated by profit, there's no reason that the initiatives need to produce anything of commercial value or result in something that appeals to consumers, yet they potentially employ large numbers of workers. If the wealthy of the future choose to pay people to write bespoke poetry for their amusement, or put on cast-of-thousands spectacles for their children's birthdays, they will be free to do so.

And that's the optimistic scenario. It could be worse—they might decide to stage the birthday spectaculars using robots, leaving the unemployed to starve. The logically extreme outcome of a capitalist economy in which the assets are concentrated within a small elite is a system wherein those at the top control everything, and the normal mediating role of supply and demand in distributing assets is no longer effective. The rich, quite simply, can literally decide who gets to work, and therefore who will live and die. All hail the new pharaohs.

But this logical extreme isn't very likely, for social and political reasons. However, as long as the indulgences of the rich aren't broadly visible, the increasing diversion of resources to serve their interests may become an ever more potent driver of our economy. A world where the masses labor to produce increasingly luxurious goods for a shrinking class of the lucky few is a frighteningly real and workable possibility.

Are there alternatives to a labor-based society?

Socialism is one possible answer, but not one that's politically palatable in today's environment (at least in the United States). In most forms of socialism, assets are collectively owned—usually either by worker cooperatives or government entities. By contrast, the private assets in capitalist economies are ultimately owned by individuals (directly or indirectly).

As work (as we currently know it) evaporates, we will need to move from a labor-based economic model to a more asset-based model. Then the problem of reducing income inequality and increasing social justice becomes the challenge of distributing assets more widely, as we used to do with land. Such a transition is not qualitative; it's one of emphasis. Today, both labor and asset economic models of wealth distribution coexist: you can work for a living or you can invest and live off the return on your investments (or, for completeness, you can simply spend assets that you control). The trick is how to get assets into people's hands without simply taking it away from others. Luckily, there are two pools of assets that are not currently owned individually: future assets and government assets.

How can we distribute future assets more equitably?

The first thing to observe is that the asset base itself is not stable. Historically, at least in the United States, total assets have grown remarkably steadily, doubling about every forty years. We are, collectively, about twice as wealthy today as we were four decades ago. For those of us old enough to experience a significant portion of this cycle, it occurs so gradually as to be barely noticeable, but is quite dramatic nonetheless.

One reason it's hard to compare yesterday's and today's standard of living is that the wealth tends to take new forms. Want to withdraw some cash from your bank account? Forty years ago, if the bank was closed, you were out of luck. Now you can access your funds through an ATM at any time. Wonder where your child is? In the past, if you had access to a phone, you could call around to likely locations and inquire as to his or her whereabouts or just wait until the wanderer came home, whereas today, most likely, you would simply call his or her cell phone or use a location-aware application. Home video entertainment mostly used to mean watching one of a small number of broadcast TV channels in real-time, while today a cable or satellite dish will deliver a cornucopia of shows and movies on demand, in higher quality and improved content. Want news? You no longer have to wait for tomorrow's newspaper to be delivered—it's available around the clock via the Internet. The selection of books, foods, products and services of every kind available to you has exploded, many of them instantly accessible. Yes, most of us are better off—not by a little but by a lot.

And this remarkable increase in total wealth isn't new: the pattern can be traced back at least several hundred years. Today's U.S. residents are approximately fifty times wealthier than their predecessors who lived when George Washington was president. So there's every reason to believe that this trend will continue, if not accelerate, given the advances in AI.

So the problem can be addressed by changing how we distribute newly created wealth, as opposed to taking from the rich and giving to the poor. Altering the "rules of the game" so that the wealth generated by increases in productivity and efficiency accrues to a broader group of people than under our current system—before it accumulates in the hands of a moneyed elite—will be easier than spreading it around after the fact.

But that's not the whole story. Government assets—essentially those that are owned by everyone—are fundamentally different from private (whether individual or jointly-owned) assets. In many cases, these asset classes are equivalent, such as when the government owns resources (for example, a motor pool of trucks) that are purchased from the private sector and can be resold to private interests. But because the government controls the ultimate proto-resource—the money supply—it can facilitate or hinder the flow and capital, effectively altering the value and allocation of effort.

This monetary control takes many forms. It can be nonspecific, for instance, when the government distributes or collects physical currency or adjusts the rate at which banks can borrow funds (the federal funds rate). Or it can be specific, as when the government issues currencies that have restricted uses, such as food stamps. The government can also strongly influence, if not control, the use of private assets by creating incentives or disincentives. For instance, permitting tax deductions for charitable contributions has the intended effect of increasing philanthropy, while early-withdrawal penalties from retirement accounts encourage saving. Or the government can simply prohibit the use of assets for certain purposes or under certain circumstances, such as making it illegal to purchase drugs without a prescription. So not only does the government have considerable control over how assets are distributed and used, it can also create new and restricted forms of assets to promote social goals. This offers the possibility of redistributing wealth in ways that are more palatable than taxing the rich to subsidize the poor.

How can we support the unemployed without government handouts?

With some creative economic thinking, we don't have to play Robin Hood to address problems of inequity. As a single—though by no means unique—example, we could take a page out of our playbook for funding retirement, applying it at the other end of the age spectrum. Suppose each citizen who survived to age five was automatically granted a trust account whose proceeds could be used only for investment. Each account could be managed by a certified financial advisor, either privately selected by the child's guardian(s) or appointed by the government. As with individual retirement accounts, only certain investments could be permitted—and perhaps also certain expenditures, such as for the child's education. On the safest end of the spectrum, these assets could be aggregated and loaned to banks as overnight funds, reducing the need for the central bank to provide this service. Or they could be invested in certain classes of securities.

When the child turned twenty (for instance), the original funds would be returned to the government, and they would then roll over for the next generation. Any increase in value, however, could become the property of the recipient, perhaps in a restricted form. (In other words, this is a limited-term, zero-interest loan.) For instance, the then current balance could be inviolable until late in life, as is the case with Social Security, while any further growth (interest, dividends, and so on) could be distributed to the recipient. Assuming this no-interest restricted loan earned an average annual interest rate of 5 percent over this fifteen-year period (from five years of age to twenty), the value of the account would have more than doubled. (For comparison, the average annual return on stocks from 1928 to 2010 was 11.31 percent.)[7]

Such a proposal has the politically palatable characteristics that it is not an entitlement in the common sense—it does not assume a particular rate of return or value, since it varies depending on economic conditions, and provides for a significant degree of individual discretion, risk level, and control (in this case by the guardian). The amounts granted under this program could vary based on the number of eligible children, or perhaps even be scaled per family to some degree. It could be started with relatively modest sums but, assuming the funds allocated to this program were to grow over time, it might eventually provide a substantial portion of the lifetime income of the average citizen. This particular proposal is far from perfect, and indeed may not be workable. However, it's illustrative of the kind of creative ideas that may help society to move to a more just and equitable future.

Why should people work if they could live comfortably without doing so?

Making a living isn't the only reason people work. While some may choose to remain minimum-income couch potatoes, many or most will want to upgrade their lifestyle by supplementing their income with wages. Others will seek the stimulation, sense of accomplishment, social interaction, and status accorded to those who strive to achieve. Our desire to better ourselves and earn the admiration of others isn't going to go away. An economic system where the worst possible outcomes aren't very severe is one that will encourage risk taking, creativity, and innovation. If starting an enterprise—whether as modest as making and selling handmade artifacts or as ambitious as raising venture capital for a disruptive new technology—is backstopped with a livable income, all of society is likely to benefit.

Also, our attitudes about what constitutes productive work may shift. Activities like caring for the elderly, raising orchids, and playing in an orchestra may accord their practitioners a level of respect today reserved for high earners. So the definition of a job—at least for the purposes of personal fulfillment and social status—may shift toward activities that benefit others or deliver nonmonetary rewards, as opposed to those that generate a fat paycheck.

That said, if some portion of the population chooses to "drop out," so be it. People are free to choose their own lifestyles, and those who opt out of working entirely will undoubtedly have an accordingly modest lowest-common-denominator lifestyle. Perhaps society will segregate into hedonistic, impecunious "hippies" and self-absorbed, ambitious "yuppies," but that's better than it bifurcating into those desperately trying to hold on to their jobs and those quietly starving to death, as has happened at some times in the past.

Notes

1. Jimmy Dunn, "Prices, Wages and Payments in Ancient Egypt," Tour Egypt, June 13, 2011, http://www.touregypt.net/featurestories/prices.htm.
2. http://www.pbs.org/wgbh/masterpiece/.
3. Matthew Yglesias, "What's All the Land in America Worth?" *Slate*, December 20, 2013, http://www.slate.com/blogs/moneybox/2013/12/20/value_of_all_land_in_the_united_states.html. See also Simon Maierhofer, "How Much Is the Entire United States of America Worth?" *iSPYETF*, October 22, 2013, http://www.ispyetf.com/view_article .php?slug=How_Much_is_The_Entire_United_States_of_America_Wo&ID=256#d1BQVb0DfpK7Q3oW.99.
4. The veracity of this story, or at least the details, is somewhat in doubt. "'How Will You Get Robots to Pay Union Dues?' "'How Will You Get Robots to Buy Cars?'" Quote Investigator, n.d., http://quoteinvestigator.com/2011/11/16/robots-buy-cars/.
5. Blue Origin: https://www.blueorigin.com.
6. The Allen Telescope Array: https://en.wikipedia.org/wiki/Allen_Telescope_Array.
7. "Capital Market History—Average Market Returns," *Investopedia*, http://www.investopedia.com/walkthrough/corporate-finance/4/capital-markets/average-returns.aspx.

8

POSSIBLE FUTURE IMPACTS OF ARTIFICIAL INTELLIGENCE

Is progress in AI accelerating?

Not all subfields of AI proceed at the same pace, in part because they build on progress in other fields. For example, improvements in the physical capabilities of robots have been relatively slow, since they are dependent on advances in materials, motor design, and so on. By contrast, machine learning is moving quickly, in no small part because the data available for training in digital form, primarily due to the Internet, is rapidly expanding. Sometimes a new algorithm or new concept sparks significant progress, but often it's the other way around—some advance in computing, storage, networking, data availability, or communication opens up the opportunity to develop novel AI techniques that exploit the advance.

In other words, much progress in AI occurs as a consequence of advances in related fields by leveraging advances in fundamental hardware and software technologies.

What is the "singularity"?

The singularity, as it relates to AI, is the idea that at some point in time, machines will become sufficiently smart so that they will be able to reengineer and improve themselves, leading to runaway intelligence. This idea comes in many variations.

Transhumanists argue that we, not machines, will be the basis of this accelerated evolution. There is a rich literature—and fervent debate—about the virtues and dangers of transhumanism, in which we will design replacements for our own organs (possibly including our own brains) or combine ourselves with machines, resulting in extended longevity (possibly immortality) or greatly enhanced senses and capability, to the point where we or our progeny could reasonably be called a new race.[1] Other thinkers, notable Nick Bostrom of the University of Oxford, focus on the need to exercise caution, lest superintelligent machines rise up, take over, and manage us—hurting, destroying, or possibly just ignoring us.[2]

Some futurists, such as Ray Kurzweil, see the singularity as something to be embraced, a kind of technology-driven manifest destiny.[3] Others, such as Francis Fukuyama, argue that it is a dangerous development, risking the loss of our fundamental sense of humanity.[4] While the idea of a technological singularity can be traced back to at least the eighteenth century (though not specifically referencing AI, of course), the popularization of the concept, if not the invention of the term, in a modern context is widely attributed to computer scientist and celebrated science fiction author Vernor Vinge, who wrote a 1993 paper entitled "The Coming Technological Singularity: How to Survive in the Post-human Era."[5] The concept serves as a springboard for several of his fictional works.

The underlying assumption behind this narrative is that there is an ethereal, perhaps magical essence that constitutes sentience and consciousness—in religious terms, a soul—that can, in principle, be transferred from place to place, vessel to vessel, and in particular from human to machine. While this may be true or false, at the very least there is no widely accepted objective evidence for this belief, any more than there is support for the existence of spirits and ghosts. The prevalence of this view in major religions is obvious, but it's interesting to note that this concept pervades secular thought as well. For instance, the idea that "you" can change or exchange bodies is a staple of Hollywood films.[6] Indeed, Disney productions are particularly fond of this plot device.[7]

Just beneath the surface in much of the singularity discussion is what has been characterized as a mystical fervor, sometimes disparagingly referred to as "rapture of the nerds"—a belief that we are approaching an end to the human era; entering a new age in which the dead may be reanimated (though perhaps in electronic form), we will transfer our consciousness into machines or otherwise preserve it in cyberspace, and a new post-biological epoch of life will begin. Anticipating this transition, some believers have started new religions.[8]

To better understand the fundamentally religious character of this worldview and its seductive appeal, it's helpful to put it in historical context. For millennia there have been clerics, soothsayers, and sects that have articulated visions of the future that are curiously similar to those of the modern-day "singulatarians." The most obvious examples in Western culture are Christian and Jewish prophecies of the return of God, heralding punishment of the nonbelievers and salvation of the faithful, who will forsake their physical bodies and/or transform into a new eternal form free of pain and want, culminating in their ascent to heaven.

The persistence of these recurrent themes has fostered a specialty among religious studies scholars—research of the structure, timing, and context in which apocalyptic visions take hold—and the modern singularity movement has not escaped their notice. In 2007, Robert Geraci, professor of religious studies at Manhattan College, was invited to make an extended visit to the AI lab at Carnegie Mellon University, where he interviewed scores of researchers, professors, and students as well as community members of virtual online worlds. He published his results in an insightful monograph exploring the principles and beliefs of those subscribing to the singulatarian perspective.[9] It may be tempting to assume that the modern movement is based on solid science (as opposed to religion or mythology), but unfortunately Geraci's work persuasively suggests otherwise. Indeed, he sees technology (in the abstract) elevated to the role commonly played by God in such worldviews, accompanied by the same dubious arguments that the coming rapture is inevitable.

While this apocalyptic narrative has widespread appeal to the general public, no doubt fanned by a steady stream of science fiction and the tacit or explicit support of prominent pundits (some of whom may be motivated in part by enhancing their own prestige or securing support for their own research), it's important to note that this perspective is not widely shared among the engineers and researchers doing actual work in AI. Many, including myself, find it hard to connect the dots from today's actual technology to these far-flung visions of the future. Indeed, the mundane truth is that little to no evidence supports the view that today's technologies signal the approach of omniscient, superintelligent machines. A more appropriate framework within which to understand the promise and potential of AI is to see it as a natural extension of long-standing efforts at automation.

This is not to say that those extolling the benefits—or warning of the dangers—of a coming AI apocalypse are necessarily incorrect, any more than those foretelling the imminent return of God and the end of the world may be wrong, but their timing and claims lack adequate foundation in today's reality. For instance, modern machine learning is a tremendous advance with important practical significance, but there's little reason to anticipate that it is a near-term precursor to creating generally intelligent artificial beings, much less the potential spark of a sudden and unexpected awakening—at least in a time frame relevant to people alive today.

When might the singularity occur?

Probably the most famous prediction is by Ray Kurzweil, who projects that the singularity will occur around 2045. His and other projections are based on charts, graphs, and statistical analysis of historical trends purporting to pinpoint a time when the relevant technology will progress so rapidly that it will essentially become infinite, or cross a significant qualitative inflection point. Others, including Paul Allen, philanthropist co-founder of Microsoft and supporter of the Allen Institute for Brain Science, take a more cautious view, arguing that evidence to estimate a date, if such a date exists, is insufficient.[10] One roundup of predictions on the website Acceleration Watch concludes that the bulk fall into the 2030 to 2080 range.[11] A more scholarly (and entertaining) investigation, supported in part by the Future of Humanity Institute, studied predictions for "human-level" AI more generally, concluding, "The general reliability of expert judgement in AI timeline predictions is shown to be poor, a result that fits in with previous studies of expert competence."[12]

Generally, the criticism of specific projections is that they amount to mere hand waving, conjuring trends from selected data or appealing to curve-fitting "laws" that are nothing of the sort, such as Moore's Law. Moore's Law is an example of a prediction predicated on what are called exponential curves. These are numerical progressions in which the next number in the sequence is the previous number raised to some power. That power can be small, for instance, when you calculate compound interest (5 percent interest increases the amount owed by only 1.05 from one period to the next). But sometimes the power is greater, such as when the number of chips on a transistor doubles every one and a half years (Moore's law).

People are notably poor at estimating the effects of exponential trends. You may have heard the parable about the wise man who asks the king to grant him a simple boon: to give him double the number of grains of rice each day for as many days as there are squares on a chessboard. About halfway through, the king has the wise man beheaded. Basically, the reason people have trouble with exponential curves is that we don't typically encounter them in nature. And the problem with doubling every cycle is that half the current amount was added in the last cycle. So if your choice of the period or the exponent is even slightly incorrect, it can cause your prediction to be wildly off the mark. To put this in perspective, imagine watching Lake Michigan fill up in an exponential progression, starting with one gallon of water the first day, then two, then four, and so on. Consider how long it would take to fill the lake. You might be surprised to learn that the task would take about two months to complete. But about a week before it's full, it would still look virtually empty—less than 1 percent full.

While there have certainly been significant advances in AI techniques, the fact remains that a lot of the improvement in machine intelligence is a result of the improving power of the hardware. On the software side, we're mostly tinkering around with various ideas of how to harness the power of these machines, ideas that have been around in one form or another for quite a while. There's really not that much that's truly new—instead we've dug deeper into the tool chest to resuscitate and polish up techniques that have actually been around for many decades. And it's far from a sure bet that the relentless improvement in computer hardware will continue its exponential progression unabated for the next thirty years or so, even if that does result in a concomitant increase in apparent intelligence by some meaningful measure.

In defense of the prognosticators, however, there is little alternative to the information they cite to support their claims, and *some* estimate, at least, no matter how speculative, is a prerequisite to justify discussion of the topic. A dispassionate view of all this expert disagreement is that the singularity, should anything like it ever happen, is very unlikely to occur in the near term—we will have plenty of warning before it occurs and thus sufficient time to take appropriate corrective action, if we decide it is warranted.

Is runaway superintelligence a legitimate concern?

My personal opinion is that this possibility is sufficiently remote and speculative that it does not deserve the wide attention it attracts. Like much of AI, the notion of machines becoming so vastly capable as to threaten humanity is so accessible and sensational that it garners more than its appropriate share of public discussion. My perspective is colored by my history of designing and engineering practical products, and others certainly have different views worthy of serious consideration. That said, there are several reasons for my skepticism, as follows.

I previously explained, when attempting to define AI, that numerical measures of intelligence are very specious. There's an old expression that to a person with a hammer, everything looks like a nail, and linear scales can foster a false sense of precision and objectivity. For instance, consider what it means to say that Brad Pitt is 22.75 percent handsomer than Keanu Reeves. Though it's meaningful to say that some people are better looking than others, it's not at all clear that attractiveness can be modeled as a flat scale. Pitt may well be better looking than Reeves in most people's opinion, but using numbers to measure the difference is questionable at best. Similarly, when we plot intelligence as a line on a graph and project it off into the future, there's a significant likelihood that this overly simplistic model lacks efficacy and can lead us to misunderstandings and poor decision making.

Then there's the problem of determining just which way a curve is ultimately trending. A given measure that appears to be increasing exponentially can easily level off and converge to a limit (called an asymptote). No matter how we choose to think about and measure intelligence, there's little chance that it takes an ever-increasing path, or at least its fruits are likely to be subject to the laws of diminishing returns.

To understand why I favor a view that the benefits of increased AI may be limited, consider a hypothetical future of Google's search algorithms. If this task were performed by some remarkably capable person today, no doubt we would already regard him or her as possessing a superhuman grasp of virtually every subject matter. And, like putative superintelligent future computers, Google search is a self-improving system, as its machine learning algorithms are constantly adjusting and updating results based on what the company's customers do after reviewing the results.

Perhaps you've noticed that Google search does a lot more than simply return web pages—it often collects information, formats it, and delivers it to you directly instead of pointing you somewhere else for an answer, as it did when the company first launched its service. Imagine some amazing future in which Google becomes as fast and accurate as is theoretically possible, quickly producing cogent, precise answers based on knowledge gleaned from the entire record of human history insightfully crafted to meet your unique needs. Over time, it learns to answer increasingly subjective questions, producing results that appear more like informed opinions and sage advice than factual statements. Which colleges should I apply to? What gift should I give my sweetheart for Valentine's Day? When is humanity likely to go extinct? Combined with rapidly increasing conversational capability, it's plausible that Google, or something like it, will basically become a trusted advisor to just about everyone. This astonishing service, offering a cornucopia of wisdom and knowledge at your fingertips, may become an indispensable tool for daily living.

But are we in danger of runaway self-improvement posing unforeseen adverse consequences for the human race? I think not. It may qualify as an AGI—artificial general intelligence—but at the end of the day it still just answers your questions. Will it want to run for president, decide to foment revolution by fabricating polarizing responses, seek to perpetuate its own existence at our expense, or decide that biological life forms are inefficient and need to be expunged? Personally, I can't see this leap from valuable tool to dangerous master without an intentional push to make this happen, or at least without our tacit consent.

Machines may be able to set and modify their own goals, but this capability is inherently limited in scope to the most fundamental purpose(s) incorporated in their design. A machine designed to fold laundry, no matter how sophisticated it is at carrying out that task and at adapting to differing conditions, will not suddenly decide that it prefers to milk cows. However, a machine that is designed to perpetuate its own existence at all costs may very well develop strategies and goals not initially intended by its creators—up to and including wiping out humankind. As the expression goes, be careful what you wish for, because you might just get it.

This is not to say that we can't design systems poorly, leading to all sorts of devastating unintended consequences. But this is a failure of engineering, not some inevitable unforeseen next step in the evolution of the universe. In short, machines are not people, and at least at this time, there's no reason to believe they will suddenly cross an invisible threshold of self-improvement to develop their own independent goals, needs, and instincts, somehow circumventing our oversight and control. The greater danger is that we will grudgingly accept some horrific side effects of sloppy engineering in order to exploit the tremendous benefits a new technology will offer, just as today we tolerate tens of thousands of automobile deaths annually in return for the convenience of driving our own cars.

Will artificially intelligent systems ever get loose and go wild?

The possibility, if not the likelihood, of systems essentially becoming feral is very real. There are examples even today. Authors of computer viruses occasionally lose control of their creations. Expunging these errant programs is extremely difficult, as they continue to copy and spread themselves through computer networks like chain letters run amok. The ecosystems of virtual currencies such as Bitcoin are not under the customary control of sovereign governments (or any authority, for that matter). They can be outlawed but not eradicated as long as they are fulfilling a need for their adherents.

How could this happen with an artificially intelligent system? In contrast to more special-purpose applications, the hallmarks of such systems are automaticity, autonomy, and adaptability. The goal for many AI projects is that they operate without the need for human intervention or supervision, make decisions independently, and accommodate to changed circumstances. If the designer has not properly matched a system's capabilities to the operational bounds of their intended use, it's entirely possible for it to escape control and cause considerable damage. As a simplified example, today's commercially available flying drones pose an obvious risk of losing connection to their controllers. To address this vulnerability, most are designed to detect an extended break in communication and in that event to home back to the precise spot from which they were launched. But the prospect of disorientation and loss, possibly resulting in personal or property damage, is one of the main reasons that licenses for such devices are severely restricted in the United States today.

But a technical or design failure is not the only way an AI system could get loose: it could also happen intentionally. Many enterprising entrepreneurs, in an attempt to preserve their legacies, have employed legal vehicles such as trusts and estate plans to ensure that their heirs do not subvert or dismantle their handiwork after they die. There is no reason that similar techniques could not be used to perpetuate an intelligent machine.

In my Stanford course on the ethics and impact of AI, I spin the tale of Curbside Valet, a fictional company whose founder meets with an unfortunate accident.[13] He took great pride in his squad of robotic baggage handlers, particularly in his clever design for hands-free management. Under a contract with the San Francisco airport, arriving passengers could check in using one of his cute roving carts, placing their luggage in a locked compartment for delivery to the airline. When their batteries ran low, the carts would seek out an electrical socket, preferably in a secluded, dark location after hours, and plug themselves in to recharge. If a fault was detected, they transmitted a message to a repair shop under contract to perform field repairs, communicating the diagnostic information and their precise location. Revenues were automatically deposited into a PayPal account, and payments for repair service (as well as all other expenses) were automatically dispatched in response to electronically submitted invoices. When the profits exceeded a certain threshold, the excess was used to order additional units for delivery and activation.

After the founder's untimely demise in a biking accident, the popular system continued for many years unattended until the airport itself was shuttered due to the growing popularity of vertical takeoff aircraft, which operated from a much smaller facility more conveniently located closer to the city. Eventually, power was cut to the airport, forcing the robotic carts to venture ever further, mostly at night, to seek out live power plugs. At first residents in nearby San Bruno were amused by these rolling gadgets that hooked themselves up to power outlets outside people's garages and decks after dark, but eventually the electrical bills, frightened pets, and trampled gardens led the town to hire a crew of robot abatement officers to roam the neighborhood collecting and disposing of the mechanical offenders.

This apocryphal tale illustrates one plausible scenario in which artificially intelligent autonomous devices can outlive their intended use and boundaries to cause unintended complications. You'll notice it falls quite short of the sort of broad, sentient capabilities that concern the singularity community.

How can we minimize the future risks?

One practical step we can take today is to establish professional and engineering standards for the development and testing of intelligent systems. AI researchers should be required to specify the operating envelope within which their creations are expected to operate, and incorporate ways to mitigate damage if those parameters are exceeded. In other words, AI systems of sufficient capability and autonomy should self-monitor their environment to determine if they are within the boundaries contemplated by their designers, or if they are receiving uninterpretable or contradictory sensory information. In these instances, they should incorporate domain-specific "safe modes" to minimize potential consequences, up to and including shutting down (though this is not always the safest thing to do), and notify an appropriate supervisory person or system. As a practical example, imagine an autonomous lawnmower that has been instructed to cut the grass within a particular rectangular space. If it suddenly determines that it is outside of that space, finds itself on a gravel surface, or detects that it is cutting down flowers, it should stop and signal for assistance or further instructions.

A related safety mechanism may be the licensing of systems by governmental bodies. A robotic lawyer may have to pass the bar exam, autonomous cars should pass driving tests, an automatic barber might have to meet the criteria for a cosmetology license, and so on. Such tests, of course, might be different for machines and humans, but enforcing a set of agreed-upon standards and identifying those permitted to engage in proscribed activities will go a long way toward eliminating rogue or faulty programs and devices. It will also provide a standard mechanism for revoking their authority to operate.

There's also a need—even today—to develop computationally tractable moral theories and principles that can serve as a fallback when unusual circumstances are encountered, or as an additional method of mitigating undesirable behavior. We may design a robot not to run over pedestrians, but what should your self-driving car do when someone decides to jump on its roof—a circumstance not likely to be anticipated by its manufacturer? A simple principle of not endangering humans under any circumstances, which it might reasonably infer would happen if it continues on its journey, may help it to do the "right thing." This does not mean that machines have to actually be moral; they simply have to be designed to act in ethically acceptable ways.

This behavioral requirement extends beyond the purely moral to the merely social. We will want robots to give up their seats on the subway to human riders, wait their turn in line, share limited resources when others are in need, and generally be cognizant of the social context of their actions. Before we unleash the next generation of artificially intelligent systems, we must ensure that they respect our customs and practices, since we will need civilized robots for a human world.

What are the benefits and risks of making computers and robots that act like people?

Regardless of whether machines can actually have feelings, it's certainly possible to create devices that convincingly express emotions. An entire subfield of computer science—affective computing—aims to both recognize and generate human affects.[14] There are many benefits, and some risks, to such efforts.

On the positive side, affective systems offer the promise of improving human-computer interaction (a field known mostly by its acronym, HCI). Systems that can sense and react appropriately to emotional states can make human-machine communication more fluid and natural. The advantages flow both ways: the system's ability to take the mental state of a user into account can be of significant value in interpreting that user's intentions, while its expression of emotions—such as bewilderment, curiosity, or empathy—can increase people's comfort in engaging with such a system, not to mention communicate important information in a familiar, easily understood manner.

But the potential of affective systems goes far beyond simply improving the utility of computers. They also serve as a test bed for the study of human emotions, enhancing our understanding of the instinctual cues we employ to decide whether an animated object has agency, and whether it is friend or foe. One classic work in the field is the highly expressive robotic head Kismet, developed by Cynthia Breazeal at MIT in the late 1990s.[15] It was designed to engage in a social interaction as a child might, reacting appropriately to a human subject's speech and demeanor. (It did not try to "understand" what was said, merely to extract the emotional tenor.) It could express delight, surprise, disappointment, shame, interest, excitement, and fear, among other emotions, through the movement of its head, eyes, lips, eyebrows, and ears. A later generation of anthropomorphic robots, produced by the brilliant artist turned computer scientist David Hanson, re-creates frighteningly lifelike and expressive versions of real people, such as Albert Einstein and the science fiction writer Phillip K. Dick.[16]

A number of projects are exploring the use of facial recognition of emotions (or other cues) and the expression of similar sentiments through the use of avatars (visual images of faces or humanoids). For some emotionally sensitive tasks—such as easing the reintegration of veterans suffering from post-traumatic stress syndrome into civilian society—the relative simplicity and safety of a therapy session with an emotionally aware avatar eliminates the stress sometimes associated with direct interaction with human psychologists, in addition to reducing costs. In one such project at the University of Southern California, supported by the U.S. Defense Department's research arm DARPA, a virtual therapist named Ellie interviews veterans in an effort to help identify psychological problems— with surprisingly accurate results.[17]

As noted in chapter 3, there is a long history in the toy industry of mechanical devices incorporating some degree of intelligence that appear to possess and express emotions. From Hasbro's Furby to Sony's popular robotic dog AIBO (the abbreviation, which stands for artificial intelligence robot, also happens to sound like the word for "pal" in Japanese), these cuddly and friendly artifacts successfully evoke emotional reactions in children and adults alike by appealing to our instinctual tendency to attribute agency, and in these cases friendship, based on one or more perceptual cues.[18]

But there are significant dangers in building devices that express ersatz emotions. If a robot that convincingly expresses feelings causes us to act against our own interests—that is, by hijacking our altruistic impulse to put the needs of others ahead of our own—we open the door to all manner of social havoc. The impulse to personify inanimate objects is very strong, particularly if they appear to be dependent on us or fulfill some emotional need. A well-known scene in the movie *Castaway*, starring Tom Hanks, concisely illustrates this danger.[19] To survive years of isolation on a desert island, he creates an imaginary friend out of a soccer ball that washes up on the beach, naming it Wilson after its manufacturer. During his rescue, the ball floats away, causing him to risk his life to save it. On the other hand, creating electronic babysitters or caregivers for the elderly that express sympathy, patience, loyalty, and other exemplary sentiments may be appropriate and desirable.

How are our children likely to regard AI systems?

Technologies that are sometimes greeted with concern and alarm by those living during their introduction are often accepted as commonplace and unremarkable by future generations. Examples include the intrusion of television into our homes, in vitro fertilization and, more recently, the tyranny inflicted by social media on our personal relationships with friends and family.

If people can become attached to their Roombas (robotic vacuums), the emotional tug of computer programs that console you when you are feeling down, give you sage love and career advice, watch over you as a child, patiently tutor and humor you, and protect you from danger may be irresistible. Today we may regard affection for an intelligent machine to be an inappropriate hijacking of feelings that evolved to bind us to our loved ones, but future generations may regard such emotional attachments as both reasonable and appropriate.

In films, the question of whether machines can be conscious or experience feelings is often answered by pointing out that you can't be sure that other humans have these characteristics: all you can rely on is their behavior. (Not quite true, but sufficient for dramatic purposes.)[20] Just as today many people recognize a moral duty to permit animals to express their inherent nature regardless of whether we regard them as conscious or self-aware, in the future we might regard autonomous, intelligent systems as a new form of life, different from us but deserving of certain rights. After all, our relationship with such entities may be more symbiotic than master-slave, perhaps analogous to our relationships with useful creatures such as draft horses and bloodhounds, whose power and senses exceed our own.

However, the important question isn't whether future generations will believe that machines are conscious, it's whether they will regard them as deserving of ethical consideration. If or when a new "race" of intelligent machines coexists alongside us, it's plausible that our descendants will feel that the moral courtesies we extend to other humans should also apply to certain nonbiological entities, regardless of their internal psychological composition.

While today calling someone a "humanist" is a compliment, if or when intelligent machines are fully integrated into society, the term may ultimately become more akin to calling someone a racist.

Will I ever be able to upload myself into a computer?

This staple of science fiction lore takes on a different cast when examined with a sober eye. A century ago, people had only tales or memories of their ancestors to remember them by, or perhaps a portrait. More recently, audio and video recordings provide a more detailed and dynamic record. If we reproduce ourselves—right down to the neural level—in a machine, is that us, or something like us? Let's just call it what it is: a machine that reproduces our memories and at least some of our mental and intellectual characteristics.

While calling it "us" may provide some fleeting comfort that we have somehow cheated death, the reality may not live up to this expectation. Being preserved in electronic form may provide the same comfort afforded by ancient pyramids to their occupants, but future generations may put it more in the category of a cherished family Bible than a living relative—something to be consulted for wisdom and advice on special occasions.

On the other hand, the level of comfort and sense of continuity it may provide could be adequate for you to think of it as "you," particularly if, as the expression goes about the challenges of old age, you compare it to the alternative.

Just as the crew of the starship *Enterprise* step blithely into the transporter, which purportedly destroys their material self and reassembles a copy out of new material at the destination, perhaps future generations will hold the view that uploading themselves into a computer is as unremarkable as changing their hairstyle. (At least until their original self isn't deactivated as planned, resulting in two equivalent claims to legitimacy.)

I doubt your distant offspring will be particularly fond of going out for a movie and ice cream with great-grampa-in-a-can, and the entity itself may experience little but pain and suffering at the lack of a proper biological container with which to experience the world, if such feelings prove to be meaningful at all in electronic form. Will this futuristic chimera lose the will to live? Will it be consigned in perpetuity to a virtual retirement home of like individuals endlessly chatting away online? If it continues to develop memories and experiences for centuries to come, what does that have to do with the original human, long gone and buried? Should it continue to control its estate at the expense of its heirs? And what claim of legitimacy will it have if multiple copies of it are unleashed, or if in some distant future it becomes possible to revive the original human in biological form?

Personally, these are concerns I hope never to have.

Notes

1. For a pointer into the transhumanist discussion, see Humanity+ Inc., an educational nonprofit that supports research, holds conferences, and publishes *H+* magazine: http://humanityplus.org.

2. For an excellent exposition of this subject, see Nick Bostrom, *Superintelligence: Paths, Dangers, Strategies* (Oxford: Oxford University Press, 2014). For a pointer to the discussion about runaway AI, see the Future of Life Institute: http://futureoflife.org/home.

3. For example, see Ray Kurzweil, *The Singularity Is Near* (London: Penguin Group, 2005).

4. Francis Fukuyama, *Our Posthuman Future: Consequences of the Biotechnology Revolution* (New York: Farrar, Straus & Giroux, 2000). He focuses mainly on biological manipulation, but the basic message—don't mess with humans or their genes—is the same regardless of the technology.

5. Vernor Vinge, "The Coming Technological Singularity: How to Survive in the Post-human Era," 1993, http://www-rohan.sdsu.edu/faculty/vinge/misc/singularity.html.

6. "The Definitive List of Body Swap Movies," Hollywood.com, http://www.hollywood.com/movies/complete-list-of-body-switching-movies-60227023/.

7. "Freaky Freakend" is a Disney compilation of shows involving the concept of switching bodies. http://childrens-tv-shows.wikia.com/wiki/Freaky_Freakend.

8. For instance, Terasem Faith: http://terasemfaith.net.

9. Robert M. Geraci, *Apocalyptic AI: Visions of Heaven in Robotics, Artificial Intelligence, and Virtual Reality* (Oxford: Oxford University Press, 2010).

10. Paul Allen and Mark Greaves, "Paul Allen: The Singularity Isn't Near," *MIT Technology Review*, October 12, 2011, http://www.technologyreview.com/view/425733/paul-allen-the-singularity-isnt-near/.

11. John Smart, "Singularity Timing Predictions," *Acceleration Watch*, http://www.accelerationwatch.com/singtimingpredictions.html.
12. Stuart Armstrong, Kaj Sotala, and Sean OhEigeartaigh, "The Errors, Insights and Lessons of Famous AI Predictions—and What They Mean for the Future," *Journal of Experimental & Theoretical Artificial Intelligence* 26, no. 3 (2014): 317–42, http://dx.doi.org/10.1080/0952813X.2014.895105.
13. CS122: Artificial Intelligence—Philosophy, Ethics, and Impact, Stanford University Computer Science Department, cs122.stanford.edu.
14. Rosalind Picard of MIT is widely regarded as the founder of the field of affective computing, having published the eponymous book *Affective Computing* (Cambridge, MA: MIT Press, 1997).
15. https://en.wikipedia.org/wiki/Kismet_(robot).
16. David Hanson, Hanson Robotics: http://www.hansonrobotics.com.
17. The USC Institute for Creative Technologies: http://ict.usc.edu.
18. Hasbro's Furby: http://www.hasbro.com/en-us/brands/furby; Sony's AIBO: http://www.sony-aibo.com.
19. *Castaway*, directed by Robert Zemeckis (2000), http://www.imdb.com/title/tt0162222/.
20. In contrast to machines, the fact that other people's biology is similar to your own is additional evidence of the likelihood that they think and feel as you do.

INDEX

ABA. *See* American Bar Association
abstract algebra, 87n6
Acceleration Watch, 142
affective systems, 150–52
agents
  corporations and, 102–3
  limitations, 98–101
  moral agency and, 105
  responsibility and, 101–3
AGI. *See* artificial general intelligence
agreements, 98
agricultural employment, 113–14
AI. *See* artificial intelligence
AIBO, 151
airplanes, 16–17
"Alchemy and Artificial Intelligence" (Dreyfus), 18
Allen, Paul, 131, 142
AlphaGo, 43
alternative dispute resolution, 93
American Bar Association (ABA), 89–90
anaphora, 62
animals, feelings and, 83–84
apocalypse, 140–41
artificial general intelligence (AGI), 145–46

artificial intelligence (AI)
  "Alchemy and Artificial Intelligence," 18
  controversy surrounding, 67–68
  generalizations and, 5–7
  hostility toward, 16, 18, 44n5
  science and, 4–7
  strong versus weak, 68–69
  success of term, 16
  terminology, 13–17
  what it is, 1–4
artificial neural networks
  brain and, 29
  conclusions about, 31–32
  layers of neurons and, 29–30
  overview about, 28
  unsupervised learning and, 30–31
asset-based economy
  future assets and, 132–34
  transition to, 132
  unemployment support and, 134–36
  to work or not to work in, 136–37
assets. *See also* future assets
  private, 133–34
  property, 103–4
assistive robotics, 51

autonomous vehicles
   car challenges, 41–42, 48n46
   crime and, 105
   defined, 50
   law abiding, 107
   licensing and, 149
   morally acceptable behavior
      of, 149–50
   restitution and, 108
   Shakey, 19

baggers, 115
Bezos, Jeff, 131
big data, 117–18
binary arithmetic, 5
birds, 16–17
Bitcoin, 146–47
Blaze Advisor business rules
      management system, 24
blue collar workers
   defining, 120
   professions not susceptible to
      automation, 121–22
   professions susceptible to
      automation, 120–21
   social interaction and, 121
   task deconstruction and, 119–20
Bostrom, Nick, 139
brain
   artificial neural networks
      and, 29
   generalizations and, 6–7
   reverse engineering of, 35
Breasted, J. H., 23–24
Breazeal, Cynthia, 151

calculator, 2
CalFile, 96
Čapek, Karel, 68
car challenges, 41–42, 48n46
cashiers. See supermarket cashiers
Castaway, 152
checkers player, 17
chess, 3, 38, 40–41

choice, 78–80
Chomsky, Noam, 60
Cognicor, 93
"The Coming Technological
   Singularity" (Vinge), 139
computable contracts, 97
computational law, 95–97
computer languages
   execution of, 66n28
   human languages and, 61–62
   purpose of, 61
computer programs
   agreements and contracts
      and, 98
   integers and, 87n11
   law abiding, 107
   moral agency and, 106
computers
   consciousness and, 81–82
   feeling and, 82–86
   free will and, 74–81
   human beings and, 7–11
   thought and, 69–74
computer vision
   explained, 54
   facial recognition, 116–17, 151
   ImageNet Large Scale Visual
      Recognition Challenge,
      54–55
   information captured and
      communicated via, 56–57
   labor and, 116–17
   real-world problems and, 56
   seeing what humans cannot,
      55–56, 65n19
   two- and three-dimensional
      modeling, 55
"Computing Machinery and
   Intelligence" (Turing), 69
concert tickets, 99
consciousness, 81–82
contracts, 97, 98
cop in the backseat, 97
corpora, 62

corporations
    liability limitations and, 102–3
    moral agency and, 106
    origins of, 102
    rights and, 105
creative intelligence tasks, 118
crimes, 105–6
Curbside Valet, 147–48
cybernetics, 13–14, 44n2

Damasio, Antonio, 81
DARPA. *See* Defense Advanced
    Research Projects Agency
Dartmouth conference
    funding of, 13
    proposal, 15–17
    symbol manipulation and, 14
Deep Blue, 40
deep learning, 34
Defense Advanced Research
    Projects Agency (DARPA)
    car challenges of, 41–42
    Ellie and, 151
    Fukushima nuclear plants and, 50
    research, 18
    speech recognition and, 59
de-skilling, 116
deterrence, 107–8
Disney, 140, 155n7
dispute resolution. *See* alternative
    dispute resolution
do it yourself law, 92–93, 109n11
Dreyfus, Hubert, 16, 18
Dr.Fill, 38
drones, 147

e-discovery, 94–95
Egypt, 128, 131
eldercare, 51
Ellie (virtual therapist), 151
emotion, 150–52, 156n20.
    See also feeling
emotionally aware avatar, 151
entertainment, 51

Equivio, 95
expert systems, 22–24
exponential trends, 142–43

facial recognition, 116–17, 151
FairDocument, 92–93
feeling
    affective systems and, 150–52
    animals and, 83–84
    computers and, 82–86
flight, 16–17
Ford, Henry, II, 130–31
"Freaky Freakend" (Disney
    Channel), 155n7
Free File Alliance, 96
free will
    assumptions related to, 75–76
    choice and, 78–80
    computers and, 74–81
    conclusions about, 80–81
    halting problem and, 77–78, 87n11
    predictability and, 75–78
    undecidable problem and, 77
    what is meant by, 74–75
Fukushima, 50
Fukushima nuclear plants, 50
Fukuyama, Francis, 139, 155n4
Furby, 151
future assets
    asset base and, 132–33
    distribution of, 132–34
    government assets and, 133–34
    standard of living and, 133
future impacts
    of affective systems, 150–52
    on future generations, 152–53
    progress acceleration and, 138
    risk minimization, 148–50
    runaway
        superintelligence, 144–46
    singularity and, 138–43
    uploading one's self, 153–55
    wild systems and, 146–48
Future of Humanity Institute, 142

Gallant, Jack, 35
Gardner, Howard, 2
general game playing, 26
general intelligent action, 21
General Problem Solver, 18
genetic programming, 38
Geraci, Robert, 140–41
gestures, 61
Go, 43–44
Goodenough, Oliver, 91
Google search, 144–45
government assets
    monetary control and, 134
    private assets and, 133–34
greedy heuristic, 26

halting problem, 77–78, 87n11
Hanks, Tom, 152
Hanson, David, 151
Harris, Sam, 78–79, 80
heuristic reasoning, 25–26
hidden Markov modeling
    (HMM), 59
history
    agricultural
        employment, 113–14
    artificial neural networks, 28–32
    Dartmouth conference, 15–17
    early research, 17–20
    expert systems, 22–24
    machine learning, 27–28
    milestones, 39–44
    physical symbol system
        hypothesis, 20–22
    planning, 25–27
    terminology, 13–14
HMM. *See* hidden Markov
    modeling

IBM, 34–35, 42–43
if-then rules, 23–24
ImageNet Large Scale Visual
    Recognition Challenge, 54–55
imitation game, 69–70

inference engine, 23, 24
integers, 87n11
intelligence. *See also* artificial
    intelligence
    AGI, 145–46
    "Computing Machinery and
        Intelligence," 69
    creative and social intelligence
        tasks, 118
    essence of, 5–6
    failure and, 4
    human compared with
        machine, 1–4
    IQ and, 1–2
    numerical measures of, 144
    runaway
        superintelligence, 144–46
    tic-tac-toe and, 2–3, 11n3
    well-defined activities and, 8
intelligence quotient (IQ), 1–2
Intuit, 96
IQ. *See* intelligence quotient

Jennings, Ken, 42
Jeopardy, 42–43
jobs. *See also* labor
    competition, 113–16
    at risk, 118–19
    routine, 117
    skills and, 114, 115–16
Justinian, 102

Kasparov, Garroity, 40
Kismet, 151
knowledge
    base, 23
    Teknowledge, Inc., 46n18
    workers, 122
Kurzweil, Ray, 139, 141

labor
    agricultural employment
        and, 113–14
    big data and, 117–18

blue collar workers, 119–22
  computer vision and, 116–17
  de-skilling and, 116
  job competition, 113–16
  knowledge workers, 122
  nonsusceptible blue-collar
    professions, 121–22
  Oxford automation impact
    study, 118–19, 125n7
  pink-collar workers, 124–25
  at risk jobs, 118–19
  routine jobs and, 117
  skills and, 114, 115–16
  social interaction and, 121
  supermarket cashiers, 114–15
  susceptible blue-collar
    professions, 120–21
  task deconstruction and, 119–20
  white-collar professions, 122–25
labor-based economy
  alternatives, 132
  land ownership and, 128–29
  middle class and, 130–32
  other systems different from, 128
  social equity and, 127–30, 132
  what's wrong with, 127–30
landed gentry, 128
land ownership, 128–29
language. *See also* computer
    languages
  codification of, 61–62
  evolution of, 60–61
  gestures and, 61
  machine learning and, 62–64
  natural language
    processing, 60–64
  statistical machine translation
    programs and, 63
  translation of spoken to written,
    4, 11n7
law
  ABA and, 89–90
  accountability for criminal
    acts, 107–9

agreements and contracts, 98
  alternative dispute
    resolution, 93
  automated systems and, 91–92
  computational, 95–97
  corporations and, 102–3
  crimes and, 105–6
  do it yourself, 92–93, 109n11
  FairDocument and, 92–93
  intelligent agent limitations
    and, 98–101
  intelligent agents, responsibility
    for, 101–3
  Moore's, 142
  overview, 89
  practice of, 89–93
  pro bono access and, 90
  programing computers to
    obey, 107
  property ownership, 103–5
  technology advancement
    and, 91
lawyer referral service, 92–93
lawyers
  e-discovery and, 94–95
  lawsuit outcome prediction
    and, 95
learning. *See also* machine
    learning
  deep, 34
  generalization and, 6
  supervised, 30
  unsupervised, 30–31
LegalZoom, 92
liability limitations, 102–3
licensing
  autonomous vehicles
    and, 149
  as safety mechanism, 149
Lickel, Charles, 42
Li Fei-Fei, 44
Lincoln, Abraham, 91
LISP (list processing), 14
Logic Theory Machine, 17–18

machine learning
  acceleration in, 138
  deep learning and, 34
  explained, 27–28
  language and, 62–64
  "New Navy Device Learns by
    Doing," 33
  origins, 32–36
  perceptron and, 33–34
  symbolic systems approach
    versus, 36–39
McCarthy, John, 1
  cybernetics and, 13–14, 44n2
  Dartmouth proposal
    and, 15
  LISP and, 14
  on terminology, 44n2
McCulloch, Warren, 32
meaning, 70–72
Medieval Europe, 128
metaphysics, 139–41
metric, 65n19
Microsoft, 94
middle class, 130–32
milestones, 39–44
military applications, 53
Minsky, Marvin, 33–34
missing person, 100–101
Modha, Dharmendra, 34–35
Modria, 93
monetary control, 134
Moore's law, 142
moral agency, 105–6
morally acceptable
    behavior, 149–50
multi-robot collaboration, 53
murder, 105, 106

Narrative Science, 123
natural language
    processing, 60–64
natural selection, 83
neurons. See artificial neural
    networks

Newell, Allen
  General Problem Solver
    and, 18
  Logic Theory Machine
    and, 17–18
  physical symbol system
    hypothesis and, 21–22
"New Navy Device Learns by
    Doing" (New York Times), 33

Oxford automation impact study,
    118–19, 125n7

Panini, 61
Papert, Seymour, 33–34
parking, 98–99
Paro, 51
Pepper, 51
perception and manipulation
    tasks, 118
perceptron, 33–34
philosophy
  overview, 67–68
  strong versus weak AI
    and, 68–69
physical symbol system
    hypothesis, 21–22
pink-collar workers, 124–25
Pitt, Brad, 144
Pitts, Walter, 32
planning, 25–27
Posner, Richard, 90
predictability, 75–78
predictive coding, 94–95
private assets, 133–34
pro bono, 90
progress
  in robotics, 138
  speech recognition, 59–60
property ownership
  assets and, 103–4
  limited rights and, 105
  self-ownership and, 104
punishment objectives, 107–9

quasi-judicial pretrial resolution
    forums, 93
Quillian, M. Ross, 72

randomness, 15
ReadyReturn. *See* CalFile
Reeves, Keanu, 144
rehabilitation, 107, 108
religion
    challenges to, 67
    singularity and, 140–41
research
    DARPA, 18
    early, 17–20
restitution, 107, 108
Reuther, Walter, 130–31
revenge, 107, 108–9
reverse engineering, of
    brain, 35
Riemann, Bernard, 5
rights, limited, 105
risk
    jobs and, 118–19
    minimization, 148–50
robotics
    adaptation and, 49–50
    assistive, 51
    defined, 49
    entertainment and, 51
    less clear-cut applications, 54
    military applications, 53
    multi-robot collaboration, 53
    progress in, 138
    R.U.R., 68
    space exploration, 50
    swarm, 52–53
Roomba, 52
Rosenblatt, Frank, 33
Rossum's Universal Robots.
    See R.U.R.
routine jobs, 117
runaway superintelligence,
    144–46
R.U.R. (Čapek), 68

safe modes, 149
Samuel, Arthur, 17
science
    AI and, 4–7
    hard, 7, 11n9
    isolation and, 18
    Narrative Science, 123
Searle, John, 16, 72, 73
self-ownership, 104
semantics, 70
semiotics, 70–72
Shakey, 19
Shannon, Claude, 5
SHRDLU, 19–20, 45n12
Simon, Herbert
    General Problem Solver
        and, 18
    Logic Theory Machine
        and, 17–18
    physical symbol system
        hypothesis and, 21–22
Singer, Peter, 83–84
singularity
    "The Coming Technological
        Singularity," 139
    Geraci and, 140–41
    metaphysics and, 139–40
    religion and, 140–41
    timing of, 141–43
    variation of ideas related
        to, 138–39
skills
    computer vision and, 116–17
    de-skilling and, 116
    jobs and, 114, 115–16
slavery, 104
smart phones, 9
Smith, Bill, 99–101
Smith, Edwin, 23
social equity
    future asset distribution
        and, 132–34
    inevitability of destructive
        effects and, 127

social equity (*Cont.*)
  labor-based economy
    alternatives, 132
  labor-based economy and,
    127–30, 132
  middle-class and, 130–32
  unemployment support
    and, 134–36
  who benefits, 126–27
  to work or not to work, 136–37
social intelligence tasks, 118
social interaction, 121
socialism, 132
software
  consolidation and, 10
  inference engines, 24
  Modria, 93
  progress related to, 143
somatic marker hypothesis, 81
soul, 139–40
space exploration, 50
speech recognition
  early attempts, 59
  HMM, 59
  problems, 57–59
  progress, 59–60
sprinkler system, 119
SRI International, 18
  Shakey and, 19
standard of living, 133
statistical machine translation
    programs, 63
status, 123
Stewart, Potter, 7
strong versus weak AI, 68–69
supermarket cashiers, 114–15
supervised learning, 30
swarm robotics, 52–53
symbolic logic, 14
symbolic systems approach
  heuristic reasoning and, 25–26
  machine learning versus, 36–39
  physical symbol system
    hypothesis and, 21–22

symbols
  physical symbol system
    hypothesis, 20–22
  Quillian and, 72
  Searle and, 72
  semiotics and, 70–72
syntax, 70

task deconstruction, 119–20
taxes, 96
taxi example, 103
Teknowledge, Inc., 46n18
thinking
  biology similarities and,
    156n20
  computers and, 69–74
  imitation game and, 69–70
  people and, 73
  Searle and, 72, 73
  semiotics and, 70–72
  simulation of, 73
Thrun, Sebastian, 42
tic-tac-toe, 2–3, 11n3
Tononi, Giulio, 81
toys, 151–52
transhumanism, 139
translation, 10
  of spoken to written language,
    4, 11n7
triangle inequality, 65n19
trust account, 134–36
TurboTax, 96
Turing, Alan
  computer programs and
    integers and, 87n11
  "Computing Machinery and
    Intelligence" by, 69
  halting problem and,
    77–78, 87n11
  thought and, 69–70
Turing Test, 69–70, 87n4
Turkle, Sherry, 51
two- and three-dimensional
    modeling, 55

UETA. *See* Uniform Electronic
    Transactions Act
uncertainty principle, 77
undecidable problem, 77
unemployment support, 134–36
Uniform Electronic Transactions
    Act (UETA), 98
unsupervised learning, 30–31
uploading one's self, 153–55

vacuum cleaner, 52
Vinge, Vernor, 139
voting electronically, 99–101

Watson, 42–43, 118
white-collar professions
    defined, 122
    least susceptible to
        automation, 124
    most susceptible to
        automation, 123–24
    pink-collar workers
        and, 124–25
    status and, 123
Wiener, Norbert, 44n2
wild systems, 146–48
Winograd, Terry, 19–20, 45n12

Printed in the USA/Agawam, MA
December 5, 2016

644292.026